Minute Taking
Made Easier

Minute Taking Made Easier

Tony Atherton

ATC

Copyright © 2024 W.A. Atherton
All rights reserved.
No part of this book may be reproduced, or stored in a retrieval system, or transmitted in any form or by any means, electronic, mechanical, photocopying, recording, or otherwise, without the written permission of the author, except for short extracts of up to five pages used for promotion, reviews, training, or personal study.

ISBN: 9798866397761

To my wife, children and grandchildren.

ACKNOWLEDGEMENTS

I was a few years into my career before someone asked me to take the minutes of a meeting. Like many others (as I learned later) I found it daunting even though I was a member of the team and therefore knew the topics well. It is even more difficult when you are not a subject specialist. Gradually I learned from colleagues and from my mistakes. Later, as a trainer presenting courses on minute taking, I learned a lot from other trainers and above all from the experiences of my delegates. Their collection of experiences, some good, some bad and some just bizarre, was invaluable. I thank them all.

CONTENTS

ACKNOWLEDGEMENTS

CONTENTS

PREFACE

1. GETTING STARTED 1
2. HOW MUCH DETAIL IS NEEDED? 5
3. WORKING WITH THE CHAIR 13
4. THE AGENDA 21
5. FORMATTING THE MINUTES 33
6. LISTENING AND CONCENTRATING 41
7. TAKING NOTES 45
8. CORNELL NOTE-TAKING METHOD 49
9. I DO NOT UNDERSTAND WHAT THEY ARE TALKING ABOUT 53
10. PRACTICE 55
11. FROM NOTES TO MINUTES 57
APPENDIX A – DIFFERENT STYLES 63
APPENDIX B – RESPONSIBILITIES 67
APPENDIX C – A SHORT GUIDE TO EDITING 69
APPENDIX D – PUNCTUATION 73
APPENDIX E – SUMMARY 77
APPENDIX F – SAMPLE MINUTES 81
ABOUT THE AUTHOR 85
BOOKS BY THIS AUTHOR 87
INDEX 89
BOOK SAMPLE: BUSINESS REPORT WRITING 91

PREFACE

The aim of this book is simple: to make it easier for you to take the minutes of meetings and write them up promptly and effectively afterwards.

The book is based on the minute taking courses that I have presented in both the public and private sectors – as well as, of course, my own experience of taking minutes. Of the over 6000 delegates who have attended my writing courses, well over 1000 were on the minutes course. Clients included Pfizer, Europol, Oxfam, NHS, the Rutherford Appleton Laboratory, local councils, social services and many others. Delegates ranged from experienced Personal Assistants to raw recruits. Generally, they found taking minutes probably the most stressful part of their work and the least appreciated.

They experienced much the same problems whether they worked in the public or private sectors, problems that I expect you will recognise. For instance, struggling with accents, not understanding the discussion, the detail needed, the jargon of both the subject matter and of minutes, people talking at once – and not understanding their own notes when they finally got down to writing up the minutes. All common issues that we discuss in this book.

Here are just a handful of the genuine comments from my course delegates; naturally, there are many more:

- *My attendance on this course will make my life easier for me.*
- *Thank you… everyone has commented on how useful it was.*
- *Was dreading today but I've gained a lot from this minute taking course.*
- *I have had very positive feedback from the attendees, who are now minuting all over the place!!! Thank you for such a successful training exercise.*

I hope very much that this book will help you as much as the course helped them.

Minute Taking

1

GETTING STARTED

'*I was told to sit in the corner. Don't interrupt. Just take the minutes.*' So said one of the delegates on a course I was running about taking and writing minutes.

This lady had been asked to take the minutes of what was to be a two-hour meeting of senior people in her organisation. When she arrived early for the meeting, she was told very firmly that she would not be sitting at the meeting table but would be on a chair in the corner of the room, and she would not be allowed to speak during the meeting.

Her story is one of many horror stories about the appalling way some quite senior staff have treated secretaries/minute takers. Because they hold senior positions it seems as if some of them (of course, I hope, a small minority) think they know best, that minute taking is a simple job which they themselves could do with their eyes shut. More often than not, the truth is that they don't, it isn't and they can't. I would love to make it a rule that no one is allowed to chair a meeting until they have taken the minutes of at least a dozen meetings themselves. But that will never happen.

I have spent a large part of my career presenting training courses, initially on technical subjects but more recently on management subjects and business writing. These have included over 100 courses on minute taking. Among the 'thanks' (which are nice) I have heard too many horror stories like the one above. I have learned from good and poor experiences, especially my own as both minute taker and chair (undoubtedly the best learning experiences) and from other people, especially the delegates on my courses.

This book is based on the content of those minute taking courses. It leans heavily on the collective wisdom of over 1000 people who have attended the courses, from experienced Personal Assistants (PAs) and secretaries to people who have never minuted a meeting before, from part-time staff to those in the full flood of a career. They work in all sorts of organisations including hospitals, local councils, government agencies, public and private companies (large and small) and charities.

Their comments over the years have helped to improve the content of the training course and many of those comments are included in the practical tips I describe here. I hope to give you the tips that have provided the most help, to most people, most of the time with the aim of helping you to produce better minutes easier and faster than before.

This book tries give you the essentials and plenty extras. Each chapter looks at a single topic and describes facts and ideas that I hope will make minute taking easier for you. Because the topics interact with one another there is some repetition; this is deliberate. It allows each chapter to remind you of related thoughts and ideas as well as covering its own subject in full. Each chapter can, therefore, stand-alone.

Of course, all of that is based on my personal choice of helpful ideas, just as you will choose the ones you believe will help you the most. If you have bought the printed book then I encourage you to mark it furiously by highlighting the suggestions and ideas you think will help you most. Turn down the corners of pages and scribble in your own thoughts. Turn it into your very own minute-taking manual.

Being asked to take the minutes of a meeting can bring a lurch to the stomach, if not worse. One lady I met was on the point of resigning because of the stress she felt over minutes not yet written up – over 30 meetings waiting to be written up all because she had several bosses and went from one meeting into another with no 'writing time' planned in anywhere. Another confessed to dreading a monthly full-day meeting for days beforehand, such was the stress she felt. For some meetings, taking minutes will never be easy, but it does not have to be as bad as it sometimes is. Maybe it can be easier than you think.

It may not be too bad at a team meeting where everyone is a close colleague or friend, but not all meetings are like that and, for that matter, not all team meetings are easy to minute. There are meetings where some people seem to talk a different language; try minuting a meeting of hospital consultants or nuclear physicists – as my delegates have.

In truth, many meetings are simply run badly with several people talking at the same time when they should not be, or even arguing with each other, whilst others are having a private chat in the corner and causing so much noise you cannot hear the intended speaker clearly. Even if you could, would you understand their accent anyway?

As if there are not enough stresses for the minute taker, a poor chair adds more seemingly without effort. In some meetings, you may not know everyone present, especially visitors whom the chair has not bothered to introduce. I've even been at meetings where, initially, it was not clear who was the chair.

You may feel a little overawed by some of those very clever people present – but do not be (easy for me to say). You are there to do a professional job in your own way and, with a bit of courtesy all round, you will do it – even if you struggle to read your own notes later.

Organisations need people to communicate with one another and meetings are an important method for discussing things and making joint decisions. However, the success of a meeting does not just rest on the discussions and decisions taken but also on the accurate recording of those discussions and decisions, with the right amount of detail (judging how much detail to include is a perennial problem for minute takers). That is your job and you may feel confident that none of the others present will want to take it from you.

Taking the minutes is one of the hardest jobs at a meeting. Let me repeat that: Taking the minutes is one of the hardest jobs at a meeting. Most of the other people there can mentally doze off for a few moments without too much of a problem, but not you.

Most of us stumble into minute taking without any training and may wonder whether we could do the job better and faster if we had some guidance. This book should help you to do that: to take accurate minutes and write them concisely so that they are easy to read and understand, and to make that whole process a whole lot easier for you.

Minute Taking

2

HOW MUCH DETAIL IS NEEDED?

Probably the question I am asked most frequently is, 'How much detail is needed?'

To answer the question, we need to step back a bit and ask why minutes are needed. Essentially, what is their purpose or what do they have to 'do'?

To answer that one, we may have to step back even further and ask about the purpose and style of the meeting. There is no 'one size fits all' where the style and amount of detail is concerned and therefore there is no single and simple answer.

Any serious meeting needs a set of minutes. Note that each individual topic that the committee discusses will have a 'minute' of its own. Collectively these become a 'set of minutes' or, more simply, 'the minutes'.

But what are these minutes for? Try to design your minutes with an end purpose in mind as if they were a tool to do a job, which they are. So how will people use this tool, your minutes? And who are those people? If you can get satisfactory answers to those questions, then you will be able to judge how much detail is needed. And you should make that judgement with the chair, not on your own.

What are minutes for?

First, they are the official record of the meeting. Whilst everyone at the meeting should take their own notes, only your minutes will stand as the official historical record, which can stay on file for years and possibly be read by people months or even years later and maybe by those outside your organisation. For some meetings, internal or external auditors, inspectors, lawyers, the press, the public and others may use them as a source document to verify that certain things were indeed discussed and actions planned. When you are at the meeting you may have no idea that one day that might happen. Now, there is a cheering thought for a minute taker!

Second, they are neutral, showing no bias to anyone. Consider a meeting between an organisation and a supplier or a client, or between management and union, or between, say, a food supplier and the hygiene inspectors, or a disciplinary meeting, or an interview, or... In such situations it is easy to see that being neutral is very important. All parties at a meeting must be able to trust that the minutes present a fair and honest record.

Third, they are a reminder to those who were present at the meeting of the outcomes of the meeting: the decisions, action points, deadlines, the names of those who must act and, to some extent, the logic of the reasoning that led to those decisions. Remember, 'Recollections may vary,' as Queen Elizabeth II said.

It is that last point, *the logic of the reasoning that led to the decisions*, that usually determines how much detail is included, from next to nothing to almost everything. We will come back to this point shortly.

Fourth, minutes inform people who were not at the meeting about what happened, what decisions were taken and perhaps whom they might need to talk to about certain matters. This could include committee members who were absent, other department heads, senior managers and in some cases the press and public. All in all, a set of minutes can be a very important document. – or not that important at all, it all depends on the meeting.

Thankfully, most do not have to meet all of these needs. So, you need to ask at least a couple of questions:
1. Who will use these minutes?
2. What do they need from them?

You need at least some idea of the answers to these or similar questions before you can determine the style and the amount of detail to include, and the style and detail will vary from meeting to meeting and, probably, from chair to chair. Simply doing what you did in your last job or last meeting is not good enough.

The level of detail needed is one of the biggest worries for many minute takers and the chair (and maybe other committee members) should help you to decide or decide for you. He or she may be more likely than you to know who will use the minutes and how they will use them.

Consider regular team meetings for example. They require relatively little detail, perhaps little more than action points. The team members were there, they know the topics very well, they took their own notes, they should have understood everything, nobody else is likely to need the minutes and they will probably be meeting again next week and can sort out any problems then. Some of the actions agreed may have been completed before you can get the minutes out. However, the chair should still decide how much detail to include as there could be other considerations.

Board meetings would be very different, as would cou[...]
disciplinary meetings, or any meetings where people who [...]
will want to see what was decided and why. For some meeti[...]
may never meet may want to understand what was decide[...]
same amount of detail for every meeting of every type [...]
appropriate. Keep on questioning, who will use them and what do they
want from them?

As well as the type of meeting and the personality of the chair, the culture of the organisation can also affect the amount of detail required. Even then, apparently similar meetings can have slightly different requirements. Here are just four examples to make that point:

- Briefing meetings to tell people things.
- Discussion meetings to explore issues.
- Decision-making meetings to discuss, decide actions and allocate responsibilities.
- Brainstorming meetings to generate new ideas.

Many meetings combine several of these aspects and maybe others too, and many have other particular variations in style. Always ask for the chair's opinion about the level of detail and maybe ask other major contributors to the meeting as well – they are your prime 'customers'.

Despite all that, the amount of detail required still comes down to the fact that the vast majority of minutes must contain certain facts:

- Decisions, deadlines and actions – in full.
- How or why the decisions were made – in summary.

It is this *how* or *why*, the logical reasoning, that determines the amount of detail and it can be a tricky decision to make – and one that the chair should help you with, maybe with some of the senior committee members too.

Designing a minute

Except for the very short style of minutes known as action minutes (which we will come to shortly), each individual minute can usually be built around a core of four things:

Introduction: The topic title and, perhaps, why it was discussed. Very short.
Discussion: The logical reasoning that led to the decision. This largely determines the amount of detail.
Decision: What is to be done? The deadline, when must it be done by? (And, occasionally, how and where it must be done.)

Action: Who has to do it?

Note that the last two, the decision and the action are often merged into a single item, often called the action or action point.

Action: What is to be done? The deadline, when must it be done by? Who has to do it?

Let us now look at each of these in turn.

Introduction

In some simple meetings where everyone understands all the topics (such as team meetings) a title of one or two words might serve as the introduction. In others, a sentence or two can be enough to say what the committee needed to discuss and why. However, remember that even when the members know the purpose of the meeting, the minutes may still need to record it.

Discussion

This provides the logical reasoning that led to the decision, the how and why the decision was made. It will usually generate most of the details and, therefore, dictate the length of each minute.

So, the big question is: How much do the readers need to know about the logical reasoning that led to the decision? At one extreme, they need to know nothing (heaven for the minute taker). At the other extreme, they need to know every twist and turn of the argument, including who argued for this and who argued for that (hell for the minute taker). More of this in a moment.

Decision and Action

As shown above, but worth repeating, some committees split these to differentiate between what has to be done and when, which they call the 'decision', and who has to do it, which they call the 'action'. This makes the *what* and *when* independent of the *who*, which is sometimes important. They then have four parts to a minute instead of, what is probably more usual, three parts.

All three aspects of the decision and action, *what, when* and *who*, must be stated clearly and unambiguously in full.

If a decision was expected but the committee did not make one, then that too must be clear. If the committee postponed a decision to the next meeting, then say something like, 'Decision deferred to the next meeting'. Otherwise you may have to say, 'No decision taken,' in which case the topic will probably reappear on the agenda next time. Even the absence of decisions must be clear.

Action points must catch the eye of casual readers who just skim through the minutes – which is what many of the committee members will do, essentially looking for confirmation of what they committed them themselves to do. Try writing the *what, when* and *who* in bold, maybe on a separate line and maybe aligned right. In many minutes, the *who* appears in a separate narrow column to the right of the minutes, a column reserved for that one purpose. (See Appendix F.)

Remember that the purpose of the minutes is to provide the committee members with the tool they want, as well as meeting any other criteria demanded by convention and the organisation. People are busy and action points must be easy to find. You have to accept that few readers will admire your Nobel-Prize winning prose, they just want the facts.

Sometimes, there can be several decisions within one topic and therefore in one minute:

A has to be done by date B by person C.
D has to be done by date E by person F.
G has to be done by date H by person I.

Each must stand out so give each one its own line, in bold and aligned right. Place each one after the part of the discussion that led to this decision.

Objective style

Some very senior committees like to have the action points written as specific objectives for someone to do, stating who is to do what by when. For example:

> *Joyce Mason to make a short presentation to the Board at its next meeting on 4 Dec to clarify the impact on the company of the new legislation.*

This expresses the decision and action in more detail and is likely to use the wording of a formal proposal (or 'motion' if very formal). Again, make them stand out from the rest of the text.

Summary: If you stick to the simple model that all minutes must have an introduction, discussion and a decision, you will not go far wrong. And the amount of detail in the discussion will largely determine the length of the minutes and for that, there is a complete range from zero to a mini essay (although few will appreciate the latter).

Verbatim, discussion and action minutes

For simplicity we can think of there being three classes of minutes. The difference between them lies almost entirely in how much detail is given to describing the logic of the discussion that led to the decision.

Type 1 – Verbatim minutes

The most detailed are often called verbatim minutes where a good introduction is followed by virtually every twist and turn of the argument. They are difficult and tedious to write and even more tedious to read. Although we use the term 'verbatim' to describe them, they are rarely truly verbatim in the sense of recording exactly everything that everyone said. (That requires a specialist minute taker.) Instead, they try to record all the important twists and turns of the logical argument (the *why*), being fair to all parties and showing all the angles discussed, followed by the decision.

Thankfully, verbatim minutes are comparatively unusual and are probably the least common of the three types (see Fig 1). The nearest most minute takers will get to verbatim minutes will be at a disciplinary meeting or a welfare meeting, or something similar. Remember, they do not record everything that was said (they are not a transcript) but they do give due weight to all the arguments, for and against. If you do have to take such minutes, try asking the chair to summarise the main points at the end of each part of the discussion or item – that is when you 'go verbatim' as he or she is more or less dictating your minute for you. (We will look at this again later.) Also take down verbatim any formal proposals (including the names of the proposer and seconder) and all decisions and actions.

Verbatim minutes will usually also be what are called *attributable*; that is, they name names, recording who made each contribution (often just by their initials), not just who has to take the action.

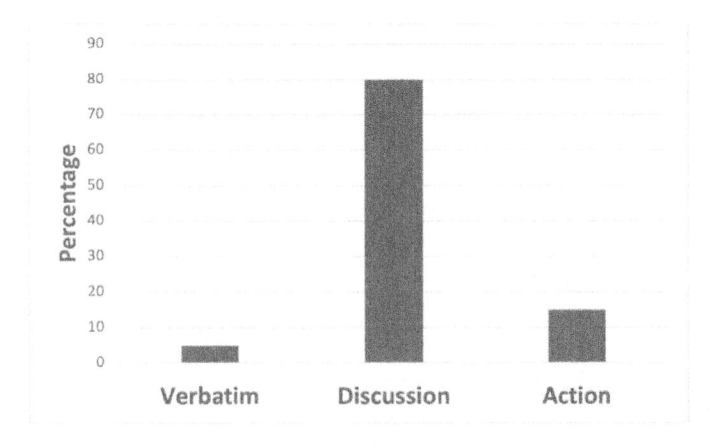

Figure 1. Relative popularity of types of minutes (very approximately and not based on measurements).

Type 2 – Action minutes

At the other extreme, the simplest minutes are action minutes and these are a delight to take. For the purists, these give a concise description of the decisions and actions. That's it! In true action minutes, not one iota of the discussion is recorded, no *why*, just what has to be done by when and by whom. However, many 'action minutes' include maybe two or three sentences giving the essence of the reasoning – no twists and turns. Action minutes are non-attributable – not naming anyone other than the person who is to take the action, except probably proposers and seconders.

Type 3 – Discussion or summary minutes

The third type is known as discussion minutes or summary minutes; they lie between the two extremes and are by far the most common (see Fig 1). The *why* question is answered; the logical argument is there but it is kept to the minimum necessary to do the job for that committee, which might be a lot or a little. Not all the twists and turns endured by the attendees because everyone had to have their say need to be recorded for posterity – restrict it to the logical flow that led to the decision. Inevitably, you will take more notes than are needed and will discard some of that information when you write up.

Although the actual discussion took many twists and turns, going here and there and coming back again, in and out of dead ends, all around the houses and maybe round in circles – the minutes show the discussion as a short and logical explanation going serenely from beginning to end by the shortest route; the perfect meeting. (See Figure 4 on page 58.)

Shorter is better

Of course, classifying all minutes as one of three types is a simplification. There is a continuous spectrum or range from verbatim to action minutes with discussion minutes occupying almost the entire centre ground and being the most common by far. Discussion minutes will vary in detail according to the needs of the committee or the whim of the chair, or just as likely, what the minute taker thinks he or she can get away with. Most experienced minute takers will try to steer their chair and committee members towards accepting shorter minutes than they might think they need. In fact, all minute takers should do exactly that.

On training courses, I strongly advised minute takers to shorten minutes (nearly always discussion minutes) whenever they can. Even when they think that will be impossible, it turns out that they can usually do it.

Minutes are usually much too long and (as already mentioned) most people just skim through them, if they even do that. For most committees, if the minutes are 20% to 30% shorter, the world will not come to an end, the sky will not fall in, but most people will be grateful (if they notice, that is). Making them 70% or 80% shorter is the challenge.

Always try to accustom committee members to accepting shorter minutes, but always keep the chair and senior members on your side. This is usually best achieved gradually as people (probably including you) can get apprehensive if they think you are going to decimate their minutes. In my experience, it is the minute takers who fear the worst not the committee members.

One of my course delegates was adamant that her committee would never, never, never accept anything shorter than the massive wedge of minutes they were used to. Later, she wrote to tell me that as she 'knew' they would never agree to shorter minutes she decided instead to add an extra page. She made them longer! The extra page was a single-page list of the action points. The committee loved it and at their next meeting they scrapped the traditional long-winded minutes in favour of a single page of action points. From a wedge of pages to just one page in two steps!

Attributable or non-attributable

One final thing to consider in terms of the amount of detail, and which has already been mentioned, is whether the minutes should be attributable or non-attributable. This simply means whether names are attributed to certain statements such as '*DK summarised the new terms and conditions...*' instead of, say, '*The new terms and conditions were summarised...*'

Attributable minutes are nearly always longer than non-attributable ones. They can become long-winded, tedious to read and have led to arguments over whether someone really said something or not. Good ideas can come from several people almost simultaneously and, if people are sensitive, naming the 'heroes' could be detrimental to team harmony.

There is a range of attribution from mostly attributable to occasionally attributable. You may need attributable statements when someone disagrees with a decision and wants their disagreement minuted. That is their right. The more verbatim the minutes are, the more attributable they tend to be. This includes disciplinary meetings, some council or social service meetings, negotiations, etc. Any meeting where fairness must not only be done but be seen to be done may need some degree of attribution.

Minutes that are almost entirely non-attributable are common in business meetings as they reduce the waffle and support collective working by concentrating on what was said, not who said it. A common approach is for the bulk of the minutes to be non-attributable but become attributable for the most important statements, such as instructions and proposals.

3

WORKING WITH THE CHAIR

Taking the minutes can be a tough job and it may be the toughest job at the meeting. However, it can be made easier if the chair manages the meeting well. If it is run badly, then minute taking becomes even harder. For example, if everyone starts talking at once, arguing or even shouting then it is impossible to take accurate notes (in such circumstances it is probably best not to try but to wait until everyone calms down and then ask for the outcome of their 'discussion'). At times, it may be in your own interests to 'educate' gently an inexperienced or ineffective chair. As we shall see later, one of the things you really ought to do before a meeting is to have a talk with the chair.

A good working relationship between you and the chair will save time and make life easier for both of you. Though, perhaps, for much of the time it does not feel like it, your relationship should be a partnership. You are part of a two-person 'management team' for the meeting, even though you are the junior partner. This is what it feels like when things are at their best. Regrettably, the partnership does not always exist. (Remember the minute taker who was banished to a chair in the corner?)

Obviously, even in a good partnership you have different responsibilities and yours extend beyond taking notes at the meeting and writing them up later. That is the minimum although there are meetings, such as weekly team meetings, where your responsibilities barely go beyond that.

Like most things about meetings, the minute taker's responsibilities vary from organisation to organisation, even from department to department, and they are often decided by the chair. Here are some of the things you may have to think about, but please note that you may not have to do all of these things for every meeting.

Before the meeting

Distribute the previous minutes

Distribute the minutes of the previous meeting well before the new meeting. It is almost useless to hand out the minutes of the previous meeting at the start of the next one. No one has had time to read them let alone check their accuracy. No one has been reminded of actions to be taken or had any chance to do any of the other things that reading the minutes might prompt them into doing. Much of the purpose of minutes has been lost. Bad practice all round.

Record corrections

Some members may have offered corrections to the previous minutes. Keep a list and tell the chair about them well before the meeting starts. You will also have to tell the committee near the start of the next meeting because the members have to decide whether to accept them or not.

Matters arising

Read, or at least skim through, the previous minutes even if you wrote them. Apart from being a reminder, you need to pick out the action points from decisions at previous meetings that the committee should be kept informed about, that is what matters arising is for (i.e. matters arising from the previous minutes, see the agenda chapter later). If these action points are likely to lead to further discussion, then you may instead regard them as agenda items in their own right. The chair should advise you.

The agenda

The agenda for the next meeting must be agreed with the chair, in fact the chair may give it to you to type up and distribute. More likely, you will write it and the chair will change a few things before returning it to you to amend and distribute. Remember, the agenda is the chair's not yours, although it is often a joint exercise. Members need time to think about items before the meeting so issue the agenda well in advance, for instance the day before for weekly meetings and a few days before for monthly meetings. With some routine weekly meetings, the agenda may be much the same for every meeting and – possibly – only unusual items need to the flagged to the members in advance.

Apologies

Record apologies as you receive them.

Board meetings would be very different, as would council meetings or disciplinary meetings, or any meetings where people who were not there will want to see what was decided and why. For some meetings, people you may never meet may want to understand what was decided and why. The same amount of detail for every meeting of every type is simply not appropriate. Keep on questioning, who will use them and what do they want from them?

As well as the type of meeting and the personality of the chair, the culture of the organisation can also affect the amount of detail required. Even then, apparently similar meetings can have slightly different requirements. Here are just four examples to make that point:

- Briefing meetings to tell people things.
- Discussion meetings to explore issues.
- Decision-making meetings to discuss, decide actions and allocate responsibilities.
- Brainstorming meetings to generate new ideas.

Many meetings combine several of these aspects and maybe others too, and many have other particular variations in style. Always ask for the chair's opinion about the level of detail and maybe ask other major contributors to the meeting as well – they are your prime 'customers'.

Despite all that, the amount of detail required still comes down to the fact that the vast majority of minutes must contain certain facts:

- Decisions, deadlines and actions – in full.
- How or why the decisions were made – in summary.

It is this *how* or *why*, the logical reasoning, that determines the amount of detail and it can be a tricky decision to make – and one that the chair should help you with, maybe with some of the senior committee members too.

Designing a minute

Except for the very short style of minutes known as action minutes (which we will come to shortly), each individual minute can usually be built around a core of four things:

Introduction: The topic title and, perhaps, why it was discussed. Very short.

Discussion: The logical reasoning that led to the decision. This largely determines the amount of detail.

Decision: What is to be done? The deadline, when must it be done by? (And, occasionally, how and where it must be done.)

Action: Who has to do it?

Note that the last two, the decision and the action are often merged into a single item, often called the action or action point.

Action: What is to be done? The deadline, when must it be done by? Who has to do it?

Let us now look at each of these in turn.

Introduction

In some simple meetings where everyone understands all the topics (such as team meetings) a title of one or two words might serve as the introduction. In others, a sentence or two can be enough to say what the committee needed to discuss and why. However, remember that even when the members know the purpose of the meeting, the minutes may still need to record it.

Discussion

This provides the logical reasoning that led to the decision, the how and why the decision was made. It will usually generate most of the details and, therefore, dictate the length of each minute.

So, the big question is: How much do the readers need to know about the logical reasoning that led to the decision? At one extreme, they need to know nothing (heaven for the minute taker). At the other extreme, they need to know every twist and turn of the argument, including who argued for this and who argued for that (hell for the minute taker). More of this in a moment.

Decision and Action

As shown above, but worth repeating, some committees split these to differentiate between what has to be done and when, which they call the 'decision', and who has to do it, which they call the 'action'. This makes the *what* and *when* independent of the *who*, which is sometimes important. They then have four parts to a minute instead of, what is probably more usual, three parts.

All three aspects of the decision and action, *what, when* and *who*, must be stated clearly and unambiguously in full.

If a decision was expected but the committee did not make one, then that too must be clear. If the committee postponed a decision to the next meeting, then say something like, 'Decision deferred to the next meeting'. Otherwise you may have to say, 'No decision taken,' in which case the topic will probably reappear on the agenda next time. Even the absence of

- Meet with the chair.
- Prime the chair about summarising.
- Book the room, equipment and refreshments (if any).
- Distribute the agenda and reports.
- Read the previous minutes.
- Prepare yourself.

During the meeting

Apart from taking notes, to which we devote a whole chapter later, what else might you be expected to do?

Arrive early and check the room

Do get to the room early and check that everything is satisfactory: the temperature, noise levels, equipment and so on. Committee members will not thank you if the data projector or smart screen does not work, for example.

Spare copies of minutes and papers

Have a few spare copies of important papers such as the minutes of the previous meeting, the agenda and reports. However important or senior the committee members are, someone will have forgotten to bring something or will not be able to find it on their laptop. Very occasionally, you may need to take reference files to a meeting. I knew one minute taker who took a trolley full of reference books for one monthly meeting.

Signature sheet

You may find it helpful to print a list of the names of the committee members so they can sign in – that will save you having to note down who was there.

Notepad, pens, pencils

Use whatever size of notepad you prefer; my own preference is for A4 (US letter size) as it offers more space than a secretarial pad. And, of course, have spare pens and pencils ready not only for yourself but for others too who may ask to borrow one.

Sit next to the chair

It is very important that you sit where you feel comfortable and able to do your job well. Personally, I feel that sitting next to the chair is by far the best spot as you may need to communicate quietly with the chair during the meeting without disturbing the meeting (that management team again). If you sit next to each other, you can whisper to one another or even pass notes; sticky notes are handy for that. You may need to explain the need for this at your preliminary meeting and you may need the chair's support to oust others who feel that their seniority or importance should place them next to the King of the Meeting. This seating is not about hierarchy; it is about roles. If someone insists on sitting next to the chair then they can sit on the other side – or maybe they would like to take the minutes? This is where the chair's support becomes very important. One of my delegates told me that she had once placed her notebook, pens and papers on the table next to the chair's place. When she turned away, someone promptly removed them and sat there himself. The chair told him to move.

Have a comfortable chair

You could be sat there for a while so make sure you have a comfortable chair. I have known of secretaries who take their own office chair to their meetings when possible. All very well if the layout of the building allows that.

Hard copy of the previous minutes

At most meetings, the chair is expected to sign (or at least initial) a copy of the previous minutes to say they have been approved, so have a set ready. At some meetings, you may be expected to use better quality paper for this than ordinary 80-gram office paper.

Check that the meeting is quorate

The quorum is the minimum number of members of a committee needed for the committee to meet. If too few are present then the meeting must be postponed or cancelled. Tell the chair if you think the meeting is not quorate.

Listen carefully and take notes

There is no need to record everything (except at certain times or in very unusual circumstances) so be very selective. We shall say a lot about note taking in Chapters 7 and 8.

Ask questions

Interrupting and asking questions troubles many minute takers but take courage. As a minute taker you may not be a subject expert. There will be times when you do not understand yet it is vital that you capture the essence of the discussion. So you need help. Imagine taking the minutes of meetings for clinical consultants or nuclear physicists. Be brave; ask questions. After a complex discussion the question you may want to ask the most is: out of all that, what do you want in the minutes? You may find that others around the table, who are supposed to understand more than you, will appreciate some clarification as well.

Even if some committee members turn out to be a bit arrogant, stick to your guns. You may be the most junior person there (or you may not) but you have a job to do and you are going to do it professionally. So, either they can help you to get it right now or you may have to pester them later, which will be far more disruptive for them. It is in their own interests to be cooperative at the meeting. Prime the chair beforehand (at your planning meeting) that you need his or her backing for this. This is where the chair can be a huge help to you.

Go verbatim during summaries

As already mentioned, the other great help the chair can give you is to provide summaries. (Sorry, but this is worth repeating many times.) This is when you go verbatim. Get every word down as best as you can because your minutes are almost being dictated to you. Ask for summaries whenever you feel you need them and, yes, I have noticed others look relieved when I have asked for a summary. They too were a bit lost.

In summary, during the meeting:

- Arrive early and check the room.
- Have spare copies of previous minutes and any papers.
- Have a signature sheet ready.
- Have a good notepad and spare pencils and pens.
- Sit next to the chair.
- Sit on a comfortable chair.
- Have the previous minutes ready for the chair to sign.
- Listen carefully, take appropriate notes.
- Ask questions. Seek clarification if in doubt.
- Go verbatim during summaries.

After the meeting

Clarify issues before people leave

Often after a meeting has closed, some people may stay for a while to chat and that is a good time to grab people to clarify anything they said that you are still not sure about. If left until later you will have to chase them by phone or email, or rely on the chair to fill in any gaps.

Check the room

Once everyone has left, you should check that the room is clear of any confidential papers that may have been left behind. (Yes, you are their nanny!). As a courtesy to others, it is normal to leave the room in a tidy state. Some committee members may be willing to help with that, although that may depend on their personality and the organisation's culture.

Draft within two days

Draft the minutes within two days of the meeting and get the chair to check, amend and approve quickly. Try to issue them within three days. It is a challenge and one you will not always meet but it really helps the committee. Handing them out at the start of the next meeting can hinder their work and is unprofessional on your part.

Unfortunately, the chair is often the main obstacle to getting the minutes out quickly. Try to explain the facts of life to him or her (easier said than done) and maybe enlist the help of other committee members if necessary. If your organisation has quality procedures for such things, then these may help you. If you are getting desperate, issue the minutes anyway and ask for corrections to be sent to you. For many minute takers that is routine and some chairs prefer it that way.

Issue papers to non-attendees

If papers are issued at the meeting, then send copies to any members who did not attend. All committee members should have those papers.

Follow up action points

In theory, the chair will follow up (chase) anyone who was given an action point by the meeting. In practice, this task may be delegated to you. That is quite normal, but it really depends on who has to act and what the action points are. Then start the whole process over again for the next meeting.

In summary, after the meeting:

- Clarify any points with the relevant members before they leave – or catch them afterwards.
- Check the room is clear and left tidy.
- Draft the minutes within two days.
- Agree them with the chair and try to issue them within three days.
- Send papers issued at the meeting to those who did not attend.
- Follow up action points on behalf of the chair.
- Prepare for the next meeting.

The Big Idea

Meet with the chair for a briefing before the meeting to discuss issues and concerns for either of you. Ask for summaries and agree a method for you to signal to the chair that you need help – probably a summary. The chair should automatically summarise at the end of every topic.

4

THE AGENDA

The agenda 'belongs' to the chair who has ultimate responsibility for it. He or she may draft it alone, with you or ask you to provide a draft for them to consider, amend and approve. It is often a collaborative effort. Whilst it is common to ask members if they have anything for the agenda, the chair can accept or reject suggestions. Perhaps the most common reason for rejecting a request is that the agenda is full and the item can wait until the next meeting.

Your job is then to make it presentable and issue it to the committee members and other interested parties in plenty of time for them to prepare for the meeting. Take care with wider distribution to ensure that you do not reveal anything confidential to those who should not know it.

An agenda is a 'To Do List' for the meeting and it has two aims:
1. To help attendees to prepare for the meeting.
2. To guide the chair and help him or her to control the meeting.

Always use an agenda and, except for very informal meetings, always issue it far enough in advance to enable people to prepare for the meeting. If they do not take that opportunity that is their problem, not yours. For monthly meetings, issue it about a week before the meeting; for weekly meetings, one or two days before is usually fine. Last minute agendas offer very little help to anyone.

Depending on the type of meeting, the agenda can range from very formal and complex to very informal and simple, with just about everything in between. For impromptu meetings, display the agenda onto a large screen or write it on a flip chart at the start of the meeting.

Content of the Agenda

What appears on an agenda can vary according to the type of meeting, the chair and even the organisation, but here are the items that appear most often on most agendas. Please note that often you will not need them all.

Purely as a guide, see if it helps you to think of an agenda as having three parts although this is not a rigorous split: the preliminaries, the core and the closing items.

The preliminaries

- Title block – committee name, date, start time and planned finish time, venue.
- Welcome (especially visitors), introduction, purpose and background.
- Apologies for absence.
- Declarations of conflict of interest.
- Committee business – not often needed.
- Approval of the minutes of the previous meeting.

The core

- Matters arising.
- Reports.
- Agenda item 1.
- Agenda item 2.
- Agenda item 3.
  Etc.

The closing items

- Any Other Business.
- Next meeting: date, place and time.
- List of reports/papers – attached, already issued, to follow, or to be issued at the meeting.
- Distribution list.

Let us run through these items, remembering that you will rarely need them all, and then we will look at three styles for agendas with different amounts of detail in them.

The preliminaries

Title block

The title block tells us that this is the agenda for committee X and it will meet at this venue on this date and time. These three items can be arranged in any sequence that seems sensible, for instance: committee name; agenda;

date, time and place. Note that it is desirable that the agenda and the minutes use the same style as far as possible so that they look as if they belong together, so when you decide the style for the title block of the agenda you are choosing the style for the minutes too.

The committee's name is self-evident but, if it does not imply the function of the committee then the purpose or aim of the meeting may also be stated.

A finish time enables people to plan the rest of their day and suggests that the chair intends to run the meeting to time.

Introduction and welcome

Either or both words can be used as the heading. The chair should welcome everybody and introduce any visitors right at the start. He or she should then give a brief introduction, setting the tone of the meeting and stating the purpose and background if this is not already well known. He or she can also stress priorities in a starting bid to achieve all of the most important business.

Apologies for absence

Strictly speaking this names only those who have sent their apologies to you in advance or have asked someone to apologise for them at the meeting. Those who simply fail to turn up may be listed as 'Absent'. Some chairs find that a bit cruel and allow them to be listed under apologies, whereas others do it to 'encourage' attendance. Let the chair decide.

Declarations of conflicts of interest

Anyone who has any potential conflict of interest concerning any of the items on the agenda should declare it now and not take part when that issue is discussed. Conflicts of interest could include personal, family, financial, etc. connections to whatever is to be discussed. As an example, a family member may work for a company that is bidding for a contract that the committee has to decide on.

Committee business or admin business

This is rarely needed and is for items about the committee itself rather than the committee's business. For example, there might be a change of membership, or a suggestion to meet more or less frequently, or a change of chair or venue, and so on.

Approval of the minutes of the previous meeting

Any corrections to the minutes should have been sent to you well before now and you (and maybe the chair) should have checked them. Members may also suggest corrections at the meeting, which is very common. The whole committee then has to check and approve the corrections. Normally, all of this is quick and free of problems.

If there is a dispute, it must be resolved before the minutes can be approved. In extreme circumstances, the approval can be deferred until the next meeting and the issue sorted out between meetings.

It is very important that the final accepted set of minutes for any meeting is correct. There must be an official, formal record of the decisions taken and this is it. Meanwhile, members are responsible for correcting their own copies of the minutes. In some cases, the minutes may be a legal document and may be used as legal evidence, for example the minutes of company board meetings and many charity trustee meetings.

If changes to the issued minutes are minor then the chair can usually hand-write corrections onto the formal set of minutes before signing them with a statement such as, 'Minutes accepted with corrections'. He or she should also initial the corrections.

At the other extreme, the minutes may need considerable editing and then be reissued and approved at the next meeting. Members should then delete stored copies and destroy any hard copies of the previous version to prevent confusion in the future. (Inevitably, some will not do that and there will be some confusion.)

Revised minutes could be identified as 'revised', ideally with a revision date or number or both. The 'formal' copy can be stored centrally on the organisation's intranet from where copies can be downloaded.

Chair now signs

Once the minutes are approved, the chair should sign the last page of the minutes before moving on with the meeting. In some organisations, the chair has to initial or even sign each page. As we mentioned above, if the chair has amended the minutes by hand, then he or she should initial the corrections as well. Electronic signatures are accepted on legal documents in many countries but check if your organisation still requires a hard copy signed by the chair.

The core

We now come to the 'meat' of the meeting; the filling in the sandwich.

Matters arising

Your role includes checking when action points are due to be reported back to the committee. Matters arising (from previous minutes) is for reporting updates on action points, usually from the previous meeting or last few meetings, that are not listed as main agenda items.

Comments should be short, otherwise make them main agenda items. Often, they report one of three things:
1. Completion of the item.
2. A brief progress report.

3. A new deadline agreed.

Although widely established, the title is not very informative and may need explaining to some people (even chairs). The purpose of matters arising is widely misunderstood and is often taken as an excuse to reopen battles previously lost. The chair should prevent that from happening.

Reports

Many committees receive written or verbal reports. Written reports are often presented with verbal summaries. Usually, reports need little or no discussion as the committee is simply being informed about something and all it has to do is 'receive' or 'approve' them. If a significant discussion about a report is expected, then make the report a main agenda item rather than a 'report'. Agenda items are for discussion; reports usually are not.

List the reports with the names or initials of the reporter. Try to ensure that written reports are issued in advance. It is unreasonable to expect people to read a report at the meeting, that wastes time. They should be able to do that beforehand. Normally, you will not need to take notes of a report, merely record that it was received or approved, but do take notes if questions are asked and answered.

The main agenda items

Now we come to the main agenda items, the discussion topics that will occupy most of the time. As we have just noted, this may include reports but only if they need discussing.

List each item separately in a logical sequence. Some committees do this in order of priority or with the most difficult items early so that if they run out of time the lower priority items can either be dealt with outside the meeting or held over to the next meeting. That means that an agenda for one meeting might look different from the agendas for other meetings.

Other committees use a fixed or traditional sequence with the assumption that the chair can take items in any order that he or she chooses on the day. All their agendas will look much the same.

As we said earlier, give each item a heading, maybe with subheadings and maybe with numbers. Usually, name the main speaker for each item (first name and surname, or just initials) and list any supporting papers.

Indicate expectations. It is very helpful to everyone if the agenda indicates whether items are:
- for information
- for discussion
- for decision
- or for some combination of these.

Sometimes the chair might issue instructions through the agenda, such as 'Seek colleagues' views.' Highlight such instructions to make them obvious so that people do not miss them.

The closing items

Any other business

Any other business (AOB) is not meant to be a free for all. It is for items that have arisen *since the agenda was issued* – not an excuse for people to raise, once again, their pet topic or slip it into the meeting behind the chair's back. Therefore, it should be restricted to last-minute items and the chair can refuse to allow discussion on any item. In fact, some chairs see AOB as a complete waste of time and ban it from their meetings.

Date of next meeting

The final task is to decide the date, time and venue for the next meeting.

List of reports and papers

At the end, list any reports or other papers that are needed for the meeting. Be clear whether they are attached to the agenda, already distributed, will follow or will be distributed at the meeting. Alternatively, this information can be included in the relevant agenda items.

Distribution list

List all those you are sending a copy to, including any non-committee members who receive the agenda for information.

Writing dates and time.

Dates

Use the same consistent and clear style for both the agenda and the minutes. If your organisation has a style guide for business writing then follow it, otherwise choose the style you think is best. For example, *12 October 2024* is a common British style whereas *October 12, 2024* is a common American style (with a comma). Abbreviating the month to three letters is usually acceptable but may depend on your organisation or committee. Using ordinal numbers (*1st*, *2nd*, *3rd*, etc.) is optional and less common than it was.

Only use the numbers-only style for a domestic readership because of the confusion between British and American practice. The date *12/10/24* means *12 October* in Britain but *December 10* in America. Always include the year, at least in the title block, as minutes are retained for up to ten years in many organisations. The international standard (yes, there is one) is: YYYY-

MM-DD or 2024-10-12.

Time

Again, check if your organisation has a style guide that dictates this. Choose a style and apply it consistently whether you use the 12-hour or 24-hour clock. The 24-hour clock is the simplest to use: *16.30* (a popular British style with a full stop/period) or *16:30* (a popular American style with a colon).

If you use the 12-hour clock, British style tends to use full stops (periods) and lower-case letters as in *4.30 p.m.*, although some just use *pm*. American style tends to use a colon and upper-case letters: 4:30 P.M. although some use lower case. Full stops/periods and a space after the numbers are preferred in more formal writing, but that is not universal. There are other variants with upper or lower case, full stops or not, and spaces or not. Consistency is probably more important than exactly what you do. The international system (ISO 8601) uses the 24-hour clock with colons: hh:mm so *16:30*, or hh:mm:ss if seconds are needed, so *16:30:15*.

Examples of agendas

A simple agenda

This is probably the most common approach to a simple agenda.

Phoenix Committee
Agenda
Monday 8 January 2024
3.00pm to 5.00pm
Boardroom

1. Welcome
2. Apologies
3. Declarations of conflicts of interest
4. Committee business
5. Minutes of previous meeting
6. Matters arising
7. Reports
8. Security lapses
9. New advertising campaign
10. New supplier trials
11. AOB

Date of next meeting
Papers attached: JS67/23, JS68/23, JS69/23.

Simple agendas like this are very common and are usually perfectly adequate for routine meetings where the same people meet every time, know the style and purpose of the meeting and discuss updates of the same issues.

However, they are insufficient for many other types of meeting. They give little information to help people to prepare. The vagueness may encourage some to sound off about their own pet issues rather than stick to the real purpose of the topics. They do not indicate the relative importance of the topics, the detail or the time needed to deal with them, nor what the chair expects the committee to do about them. They do not name the principal speakers and do not refer to any supporting papers or reports. Consequently, many meetings need more detailed agendas. Also, they may or may not have a distribution list.

In the example above, all the items are numbered but many agendas do not use numbers. It is a small matter but the chair may have a preference. Some people find it helpful to refer to items by number.

A more detailed agenda

The following example adds much more detail to guide the committee.

Phoenix Committee

Agenda

Monday 8 January 2024
3.00pm – 5.00pm
Boardroom

1. Welcome.
2. Apologies for absence.
3. Declarations of conflicts of interest.
4. Committee business: New HR representative – for information.
5. Minutes of previous meeting (4 Dec 2023). Distributed 6 Dec 2023 (AW/HM35/23).
6. Matters arising.
    a. Burnham Road office move – John Edwards.
    b. Age discrimination legislation – Mary Gaiter.
    c. New branding progress – Hilary Smeedon.
7. Reports.
    a. Financial update – Alice Jacobs – for information (AJ17/23 already distributed).
    b. Renewal of the travel agency contract – Hilary Smeedon – for approval (HS1/24 already distributed).

8. Reduction of security lapses – Karl Stephens (KS2/24 already distributed) – for decision.
9. New advertising campaign – Hilary Smeedon – for discussion.
10. New supplier trials – Jon Spencer – for discussion and decision.
    a. Car leasing.
    b. Stationery supplies.
    c. Catering.
11. Any other business.
Date of next meeting.
Papers attached (JS67/23, 68/23, 69/23).
Distribution list: A, B, C…

This is probably the most common approach. The added details give far more guidance to the committee including telling the committee what it is expected to do with items 7 to 10. Again, all the items are numbered although many agendas do not use numbers.

Someone once suggested that the main agenda items (which will occupy most of the committee's time) should be emphasised in some way, perhaps appearing in italics or bold, or being separated from the rest by line spaces. Personally, I have never done that but some people may like the idea.

Notice that the three papers distributed with the agenda are listed at the end, whereas those already issued are with their relevant agenda item. Neither approach is right or wrong but item 10 could have been written as:

10. New supplier trials – Jon Spencer – for discussion and decision.
    a. Car leasing. JS67/23 attached.
    b. Stationery supplies. JS68/23 attached.
    c. Catering. JS69/23 attached.

An objectives-style agenda

Some organisations like to go further and use an objective style, where many items state specifically what the committee must do. Again, the detail can vary but there is no point is providing too much.

Phoenix Committee
AGENDA

Monday 8 January 2024
3.00pm – 5.00pm
Boardroom

1. Welcome.
2. Apologies for absence.

3. Declarations of conflicts of interest.
4. Committee business: To welcome Mary Gaiter, the new HR representative.
5. Minutes of previous meeting.
   To approve the minutes of the meeting held on 4 Dec 2023, distributed 6 Dec 2023 (AW/HM35/23).
6. Matters arising.
   a. Burnham Road office move (John Edwards).
   b. Age discrimination legislation (Mary Gaiter).
   c. New branding progress (Hilary Smeedon).
7. Reports.
   a. To receive the financial update (Alice Jacobs, AJ17/23 already distributed).
   b. To approve the proposal from Hilary Smeedon to renew the travel agency contract for three years. (HS1/24 already distributed.)
8. Reduction of security lapses (Karl Stephens). To decide what actions to take. (KS2/24 already distributed).
9. New advertising campaign (Hilary Smeedon). To consider outline ideas for the new campaign.
10. New supplier trials (Jon Spencer).
    a. To confirm the decision on the new car leasing trial. (JS67/23 attached)
    b. To choose a new stationery supplier. (JS68/23 attached)
    c. To consider proposals for a new catering supplier and decide who to invite for a trial. ((JS69/23 attached).
11. Any other business.

Date and place of next meeting. Monday 5 February 2024 at 3.00pm in the Boardroom.

Comment

As you can see, there are a lot of variables and to some extent you can mix and match as you see fit except that what you do may be dictated by the type of meeting and the chair's preferences. Also, bear in mind that if your organisation has a guide that specifies a style then you should follow it. For example, a town council that publishes its minutes on the web will probably want all their minutes to have the same style. So, if you have a style guide – follow it!

Even the layout can vary. For example, in the header it does not really matter whether you put 'Agenda' at the top or the committee's name at the top. Paragraphs are usually aligned left or tabbed in from the subtitles, but preferably not centred. Go with what seems sensible and what people are happy with – provided the details are clear.

Remember that, wherever possible, it is usually good to identify items as 'for information' (i.e. not for discussion and no decisions expected), 'for discussion' (but a decision is not expected), or 'for decision' or a combination.

In summary, the style of the agenda is largely up to you and the chair unless dictated by the organisation. It should reflect the nature of the meeting. The three styles shown here, simple, detailed and objectives are all commonly used and there are variations on each theme and hybrids between them. Discuss these style issues with your chair and perhaps with senior members of the committee before deciding which approach to take, which might be different for different committees.

Some notes

Punctuation

Agendas can be punctuated in many ways and it is not the most important point to worry about. A common trend is to omit full stops (periods) at the end of each item. However, including full stops makes the agenda look more professional, or you may decide to use full stops only at the end of proper sentences. Consistency is more important than what you do, within reason.

Sentence case

Whether to use sentence case as in 'New supplier trials' or initial capitals, as in 'New Supplier Trials' is a matter of choice. See which your chair prefers.

Estimated times

Some committees like to see estimated times on the agenda as they give them at least some idea what is expected. Also, you can use them to help the chair keep roughly to time. Although predicting the times is notoriously difficult, some chairs like to use them to manage the meeting. If you do use estimated times then choose between stating the estimated duration of each item (e.g. 10 mins, 20 mins) or giving the estimated start times for each item (e.g. 10.30, 10.40).

Finally, here are a few useful words for agendas: agree, approve, choose, confirm, consider, decide, discuss, endorse, explore, receive, recommend, report, resolve, propose (or if very formal, 'move' a 'motion'), second, etc.

5

FORMATTING THE MINUTES

The format for most minutes is broadly similar, although of course the details can vary. However, where you can, for instance in the title block, try to keep the style similar to the one you used for agenda so that they look as if they belong together.

Example

The example below shows one approach and includes most things that can occur in minutes, although you may not need everything shown here.

Phoenix Committee
MINUTES
Monday 8 January 2024
3.00pm
Boardroom

Present
    Ann Walker, Head of Division – Chair
    John Edwards, Project Manager
    Karl Stephens, Principal Engineer
    Jon Spencer, Facilities Manager
    Hilary Smeedon, Head of Marketing
    Mary Gaiter, HR
    Alice Johnston, Senior Engineer
    Harry Martin, Operations Manager and Secretary

In attendance
    Alun Davies, HR – items 1-6
    Alice Jacobs, Finance – item 7 only
    Helen Brightway, Quality Assessor – items 8-10

Observers
Alex Jenkins (Company Secretary)
Press (1), Public (3) – item 9 only.

1. **Welcome**
   The chair welcomed Mary Gaiter to the committee, and Alex Jenkins and Alun Davies to the meeting.
   Purpose: To review progress of the major change programme, Project Phoenix.
2. **Apologies**
   Charles Spencer, Engineer
   Absent
   Graham Gloss, Finance
3. **Declarations of financial interest**
   None declared.
4. **Committee business**
   Mary Gaiter joined the committee, replacing Eric Smyth as the HR representative.
5. **Minutes of previous meeting** (4 December 2023, AW/HM35/23.)
   The minutes were approved after the following amendment: '4.1 Presentation made by Nathan Ellery of G.C. Collier Ltd.'
6. **Matters arising**
   a. Burnham Road office move: Completed, John Edwards.
   b. Age discrimination legislation: In hand, Mary Gaiter.
   c. New branding progress: New deadline, 18 March 2024. Hilary Smeedon.
7. **Reports**
   a. Financial update from Alice Jacobs was received (AJ17/23).
   b. Proposal from Hilary Smeedon to renew the travel agency contract for three years was approved (HS1/24).
8. **Reduction of security lapses**
   A written proposal from Karl Stephens (KS2/24), seconded by Jon Spencer, was accepted unanimously in full. The first two action points are to be completed by 1 February and a timetable for the remaining eight to be submitted to the next meeting.
   Action: Karl Stephens by 1 Feb 2024
9. **New advertising campaign**
   Three prototype versions of the campaign were presented and discussed. Jon Spencer proposed that versions A and C be developed for a final decision at the next meeting. Seconded by Hilary Smeedon. Carried: for 7, against 1.
   Action: Hilary Smeedon by 5 Feb 2024

10. **New supplier trials**
    a. **Car leasing.** The previous provisional decision to award the new car leasing contract to ABC Vehicles for five years was confirmed. Proposed by Jon Spencer, seconded by John Edwards and carried unanimously. (JS67/23)
       Action: JS by 5 Feb 2024
    b. **Stationery supplies.** Jon Spencer outlined three bids for the new stationery contract and proposed accepting the bid from D Stationery. Seconded by Alice Johnston and carried unanimously. (JS68/23)
       Action: JS by 5 Feb 2024
    c. **Catering.** Jon Spencer outlined the main requirements to be met by the new catering contractor and described the strengths and weaknesses of each bidder. He explained that supplier E had little experience of dealing with such a large contract whereas both F and G had considerable experience and good reputations, as described in the paper distributed before the meeting. Mary Gaiter proposed that further discussions be held with F and G and bids be invited ready for the next meeting when one could be chosen for a trial. Seconded by John Edwards and carried unanimously. Ann Walker asked Mary Gaiter to accompany Jon Spencer when visiting F and G. (JS69/23)
       Action: JS and MG by 5 Feb 2024
11. **Any other business**
    Alice Johnston reported a conversation with a senior engineer at H Consultants, whom she had met at an engineering institute gathering. They have been running a successful major change programme over the last 18 months and had learned a lot from mistakes they had made. She suggested approaching them to see what we could learn from them. This was approved and John Edwards was asked to join Mary if any visits were arranged.
       Action: AJ and JE by 8 Feb 2024

Meeting closed at 5.15pm.
Date of next meeting: 5 Feb 2024 at 3.00pm in the Boardroom.

Comments

Numbering

In the last chapter, we suggested numbering the items in the agenda. Whilst helpful in an agenda, numbering the minutes can be very helpful indeed. It provides an infallible reference to each individual minute. You can restart from '1' for each new set of minutes but it is even more useful to number sequentially through the whole year, regardless of whether you number everything (from the welcome to any other business) or only the main agenda items.

For committees that continue for several years (such as board meetings) consider prefixing the number with the first two digits of the year, thus giving a unique number to every single minute of every meeting over decades (e.g. 05/241, 16/65, 24/12 etc.). This number can appear with the title as normal or could be in a separate narrow column on the left. If this system had been used above, then item 14 would have looked like this (you can leave the cell border lines in or remove them):

24/9	**New advertising campaign.** Three prototype versions of the campaign were presented and discussed. Jon Spencer proposed that versions A and C be developed for a final decision at the next meeting. Seconded by Hilary Smeedon. Carried: for 7, against 1. **Hilary Smeedon by 5 Feb 2024**

If you like, you can match the numbering to that on the agenda. To do this you may need to avoid numbering the list of those present, those in attendance, etc., which are not actually minutes themselves.

Verbs and pronouns
Use the past tense. Write in the third person and be specific when referring to people, departments and organisations. Only use the pronouns *we, our, they* etc. once it is clear whom you are referring to.

How long should minutes be retained?
It is very important that you check your organisation's rules about this as there is no universal rule. Some minutes are more ephemeral than others. Some can be disposed of after a few months, others must be held for many years. For example, usually the minutes of team meetings can be disposed of when no longer of any practical use (as long as the organisation does not say otherwise) whereas by law the minutes of Board Meetings must be kept for ten years in the UK and seven years in many American states. Some minutes have to be kept permanently. For example, the minutes of Church of England Parochial Church Council (PCC) meetings should be deposited with the local Records Office for permanent storage when no longer needed by the church.

(Note: This is not legal advice as I am not qualified to give legal advice. Check the rules for your organisation.)

Section by section
Heading
Use the same style as for the agenda.

Purpose
This is rarely needed. Use it if it helps people, such as when the committee's name is almost meaningless as in 'Phoenix Committee', whereas names like 'Health and Safety Committee' or 'Finance Committee' need no explanation.

Present
Always list the attendees. State their job title and status or role as not everyone who looks at these minutes, either now or in the future, will know who all these people are. Put the chair first, your own name last (but see 'In attendance' below) and other attendees in the most appropriate order. This may be alphabetical order, by seniority, by affiliation or department and so on. 'Present' is usually the term used in more formal minutes but sometimes other terms, such as 'Attendees', are used. You do not need to use a vertical list as above, an in-text list is fine. For example:

> **Present:** Ann Walker, Head of Division – Chair; John Edwards, Project Manager; Karl Stephens, Principal Engineer; Jon Spencer, Facilities Manager; Hilary Smeedon, Head of Marketing; Mary Gaiter, HR; Alice Johnston, Senior Engineer; and Harry Martin, Operations Manager and Secretary

In attendance
This is for people who are not members of the committee, such as visitors and, quite possibly, you. For example, a management accountant or HR representative may sit in on a team meeting but would not be a member of that team. If you, the minute taker, are not a member of the committee (i.e. you cannot vote) then, strictly, your name should be under 'In attendance'. If you are a member of the committee then your name comes at the end of the 'Present' list.

'In attendance' is often ignored for less formal meetings (everybody's name being under 'Present') but it should be used in formal meetings.

Part-time attendance
The minutes should distinguish who attended the whole meeting and who was there for only part of it. Probably the neatest way to identify those who were there for only part of the meeting is to put something like 'Items 3-5 only' or 'Items 3 to 5 only' after their name and job title. True, they might have heard part of the end of the conversation about item 2 and maybe the start of item 6 but that usually does not matter. If it does then more precision is needed, so state within the minutes themselves something like, 'Alice Jacobs joined the meeting' and 'Alice Jacobs left the meeting'. Whilst precise, it is a bit cumbersome.

Apologies
Strictly, this should only be used for those who have sent their apologies,

even if someone else gave them at the start of the meeting.

Absent
Names and shames those who failed to turn up and did not send their apologies. Whilst not often used, it can help new chairs to stamp their authority on a committee.

Observers
Occasionally some meetings, council meetings for example, may have observers present such as media reporters or members of the public. Normally, just give the numbers of each type who were there.

Declarations of financial interest
Anyone who declares a financial interest in any item should not take part in the discussion about that item and must not vote on it. In some organisations, they may be required to leave the room until the discussion of that item is finished.

Sequence of items
Follow the agenda's sequence regardless of what happened at the meeting.

Committee business
Can be called 'Administration' and is solely for business about the committee itself, such as changing the frequency of the meetings, introducing a new member, etc.

Approval of previous minutes
This should always happen and you should always record it. In a sense, the minutes are only your offer of minutes until the committee approves them when they become the official minutes of the previous meeting.

Corrections to previous minutes
There is always the possibility of a mistake in your minutes and committee members are expected to check them and tell you if they think there is a mistake. Most will focus on the parts that are closest to their hearts. Their comments will probably be accurate, although we cannot rule out the possibility that someone will try to get something changed simply because they do not like it, even if it is correct.

Corrections usually appear in the minutes of the meeting after the one in which the mistake was made. Your job (between meetings) is to note any suggestions for corrections as they come in, tell the chair and (at the next meeting) tell the committee. The members then decide whether to accept the corrections, which they usually do. If they do, you then note the corrections in the minutes of this current meeting. Therefore, if there was a mistake in, say, the minutes of the December meeting, the correction will not appear in print until the minutes of the January meeting.

This time lag is unfortunate as it poses the risk that someone who reads a set of minutes could be misled by missing a mistake because they have not checked *the next set of minutes* to look for any possible correction. You can eliminate this risk if you post your minutes on an intranet or website. You can initially post and identify your minutes as 'not yet approved' and, after any corrections, show them as 'approved'. Of course, such an approach must be agreed with your chair.

When showing the corrections in the next set of minutes, do this in any way that is clear and the committee is happy to accept. Exactly how to do it could be debated endlessly and with little value. Whatever approach you take, agree it with the chair and be consistent. In the example above, underlining the name 'Ellery' implies that it was misspelled in the original. Another way is to say, 'Change 'Elery' to 'Ellery'.

Substitutions

If a committee member, say Brian Smith, cannot attend for whatever reason, he may send a substitute, say Alice Brown, and this must be recorded in any way that seems sensible. For example: 'Alice Brown, representing Brian Smith'.

Matters arising

As noted earlier, 'Matters arising' is for reporting updates on action points from the previous meeting or meetings – and they should be restricted to this. Ideally, the comments will merely confirm that the action has been completed, in which case record it as 'Completed'. Sometimes it is not quite complete and a little more work is needed, in which case record it as 'In hand'. In other cases, maybe not much progress has been made and a new deadline is agreed, in which case record the new deadline. If an item for matters arising is expected to need much discussion, move it to the main agenda and number it.

As already mentioned, although widely established, the term 'matters arising' is not very informative and its purpose is widely misunderstood. It is often taken as an excuse to reopen battles previously lost. The chair must prevent that.

Some meetings consist almost entirely of matters arising, that is they are mainly updates of actions taken since the last meeting and this may go on for meeting after meeting. The same items occur every time and often include discussions. Chairs are then likely to scrap matters arising and make everything main agenda items with numbers.

Reports

Check with the chair but it is quite common to record very little about reports in the minutes as they are not for debate by the committee, just to tell them something. For you, it should be as simple a job as recording something like, 'received' or 'approved' for each report in turn.

Action points

As noted earlier, these must be recorded very clearly as many readers just look for the action points. They must stand out on the page. One approach, as above, is to record the name of the person and the date on a separate line after the minute, in bold and right aligned. Another popular approach is to use a separate narrow column on the right edge of the page for the initials of the person and the deadline or reporting date. Using this approach, item 14 above would have looked like this (Appendix F shows another example):

24/9 New advertising campaign. Three prototype versions of the campaign were presented and discussed. Jon Spencer proposed that versions A and C be developed for a final decision at the next meeting. Seconded by Hilary Smeedon. Carried: for 7, against 1.	**Hilary Smeedon by 5 Feb 2024**

Using three columns can work well, like this:

24/9	**New advertising campaign.** Three prototype versions of the campaign were presented and discussed. Jon Spencer proposed that versions A and C be developed for a final decision at the next meeting. Seconded by Hilary Smeedon. Carried: for 7, against 1.	**Hilary Smeedon by 5 Feb 2024**

Again, you can delete the border lines or leave them in. Use the table facility in your word processor rather than the column facility. For comparison, it looks like this without the borders. Which do you prefer?

24/9   **New advertising campaign.**
        Three prototype versions of the campaign were   **Hilary**
        presented and discussed. Jon Spencer proposed   **Smeedon**
        that versions A and C be developed for a final   **by 5 Feb**
        decision at the next meeting. Seconded by Hilary   **2024**
        Smeedon. Carried: for 7, against 1.

The specific objective approach may be needed for the minutes of more senior committees, recording in full in sentences who has to do what by when.

24/9   **New advertising campaign.**
        Hilary Smeedon to develop versions A and C for a final decision at the next meeting on the 5 Feb 2024. Proposed by Jon Spencer, seconded by Hilary Smeedon. Carried: for 7, against 1.

6

LISTENING AND CONCENTRATING

It is a sad fact that most of us are not naturally good listeners. Eavesdrop any conversation and you will find that most people tend to do more talking than listening and generally miss or ignore some comments that might actually be important to the speaker. If someone starts to tell us about their bad back then we very quickly start to tell them about our bad back, or someone else's bad back, as if that will help them. This, of course, is the ordinary ebb and flow of a perfectly natural conversation but it is not what a minute taker should be doing when listening at a meeting. Listening for minute taking is quite different.

Whilst not naturally good at listening, we are inherently even worse when listening to topics that we find boring and that go on for a long time – like many of the meetings we might have to attend and minute. Therefore, it is important to make a big effort to concentrate and listen well when taking minutes. It is our job and it is hard work.

However, the good news is that listening skills can be improved if we work at them. In fact, we should deliberately try to improve our listening skills specifically for minute taking. Here are some ideas that have helped others. They are divided into the three categories: ideas for yourself, ideas about the environment and ideas for your guardian angel(!) – the chair.

For yourself

Practise! Practise concentrated listening and filtering. Every skill you have ever learned from walking, talking and feeding yourself has been improved by practice. This is the obvious way to improve your listening skills.

Try listening attentively to factual television and radio programmes, such as news broadcasts and documentaries. Do not take notes to begin with, you can do that later. Instead, just practice listening carefully and sorting out the wheat from the chaff, getting to the basic story they are telling. You will gradually get better at differentiating between the crux of the story and the peripherals – and even the padding if there is any. Once you are really good at accurately isolating out the main story, then start to identify the most important peripherals. Work at it until you are able to summarise the main messages in your own words. Then move on to taking notes (see the next chapter).

What you are doing is filtering what matters most from what matters much less or not at all. Filtering is one of the most important skills to develop. Not everything is important. Filtering the important from the not important requires continuous concentration and focussed listening. Surprisingly, even if you do not understand the topic, you can still filter to some extent. (The chair's precious summaries should carry you the rest of the way.)

When people try to explain things at a meeting, they use far more words they would if they had been able to prepare properly. We all do it because in our minds we are trying to sort out what we want to say whilst saying it and that does not lead to succinct and memorable speeches. As minute takers, we should try to find the meaning of what is being said rather than focussing entirely on the specific words. It is not easy but you do not need to be perfect at doing it, just better or even much better than you are naturally. Practice will help to improve your skill.

Also, listen for clues about where the speaker is heading: first, next, finally, however, on the other hand and so on. These introduce changes in the speaker's flow. Sometimes they can be misleading such as when someone says, 'There are three main points,' but then gives only two, or four. Also listen for words such as, definitely, possibly, essential and so on.

Do not scribble down everything that is said, hoping to sort it all out later. That is perhaps the biggest trap to topple into. Not only is it exhausting and unnecessary (except at certain times which we will mention later) but it leaves you with a mass of almost indecipherable notes to untangle later. This is not really listening in the active sense of differentiating between what is important and what is not important. Up to a point, you can scribble away without having a clue about what they are talking about; as a university student I was pretty good at that but it did not help me much.

If you can, learn a little more about topics you are going to meet regularly. A little knowledge may well be a dangerous thing but knowing something and some of the jargon is helpful when you are trying to figure out what matters and what does not.

Recognise when your mind wanders and drag it back. The fact that your mind wanders occasionally when taking notes means that you are a perfectly normal human being. However, as your notes are the ones that matter most (although you can always seek help after the meeting if you miss something) try to force yourself back when your mind does wander. Most of us get into a panic and we seem to think we have missed several minutes of the most important things ever said at any meeting – which is extremely unlikely. When your mind does suddenly return to reality, simply leave a big space in your notes (say two inches or five centimetres, or more, so that it is unmistakable later) and scribble down the initials or name of the speaker. Then restart where the meeting now is.

Do not search your brain for what you missed. Sometimes, we seem to feel that if we chase through our brain energetically enough we will somehow catch up with the missing information as if it is roaming around in there looking for somewhere to pitch camp. It never works and simply means we miss even more information. Leave that big space in your notes and let the chair's summary provide the missing link; if it does not do so then it was probably of little consequence anyway.

Later, check to see if the sense of the notes you took before the loss of concentration flows serenely into the sense of the notes you took when you came to. If it does, probably there is no problem; if it does not then maybe you missed something but it does not appear to have been important if the chair omitted it in the summary. You can always ask the speaker or the chair later.

Ignore distractions, such as what is going on outside the window, the coffee arriving, etc. When the coffee arrives it is natural to mentally break off and most people will do that, except perhaps the person who is speaking – stick with them (although they will probably have to repeat whatever they were saying).

Take a break when the refreshments arrive. The others will usually take a short break so try to do the same. It is tempting to chase people for clarification and end up with the meeting restarting before you have had a rest. This has to be a personal decision, to chase or to rest. Preferably, take a break and then ask for clarification when the meeting restarts – something else to brief the chair about in your planning meeting.

Remember, you are the minute taker not the waiter or waitress, so do not serve the coffee. If they look to you to do that, then remain seated and stare hard at your notes until they decide to help themselves – then get your coffee too.

Meanwhile, always have a drink available. Many people suggest that water is the best drink to help with concentration but: your drink; your choice.

About the environment

Your environment can affect how easy or difficult it is for you to do your job so try to eliminate, or at least limit, obstacles to concentration such as a noisy or stuffy room or noisy surroundings. If things are really bad then you may have to change rooms, although that may be impossible at the last minute.

Do not face towards potential distractions. Yes, the chances are that whatever is going on outside the window is far more interesting that what is happening inside the room – but you have to focus on the latter not the former.

Get a comfortable chair. You could be sat on it for a couple of hours or more. I have known minute takers wheel their own chair into a meeting room. Obviously, that is not always practical.

Make sure that you can see all the people, it helps when listening to them.

For the chair

We will keep repeating this one: politely ask the chair beforehand to be sure to give those essential summaries. If you get anxious about taking minutes then you are not alone, many minute takers (perhaps most) feel that way. Some tell me that they feel very junior compared to all those mighty people; they feel nervous about their role. Such feelings are not easy to overcome but you can feel a lot more confident if you know the chair will support you, especially by giving those summaries.

Ask the chair to enforce a rule of 'one speaker at a time' if that is appropriate for the type of meeting. When several people are talking at the same time it is almost impossible to take minutes anyway. Who should you follow? You will not be the only one struggling to unravel the conversation and the chair must sort this out. At some meetings (brainstorming meetings, for example) it is part of the way the meeting works. In such cases, your job is actually simplified! You can sit back, take a short break, and wait until the free for all is over when you or the chair can ask for the outcome of the discussion.

7

TAKING NOTES

Your notes are your keys to success, the basis of your minutes. Whilst you can check misunderstandings after the meeting, it is obviously much better to get things right during the meeting than have to chase people afterwards.

As mentioned in the previous chapter, much of this is about filtering. One of the key skills of the good note taker is the ability to filter, to be selective, recording in detail the important things and recording nothing – or very little – of things that have little importance. You need good judgement, so get the chair's help if necessary. Practise at home with news broadcasts as already mentioned.

Discussions often wander, only gradually producing a coherent argument. The well-known Pareto or 80:20 rule gives us an insight into what meetings are like. The 80:20 rule simply states that things in life are not equal, that relatively few of the things that happen (say around 20%) give us a disproportionate amount of what matters (say around 80%). It is often used to express wide generalisations such as: 20% of a business's customers provide 80% of the turnover; 20% of criminals commit 80% of crime, 20% of staff produce 80% of personnel problems and so on. Of course, the 20% and 80% numbers are very approximate.

Applied to meetings it suggests that a relatively small proportion of what is said contains the bulk of what matters and a relatively large proportion of what is said produces only a little that matters. Now, does that sound true to you? Does it give you some reassurance? Remember, you mainly want the destination and maybe the key turns along the way, but not every twist and turn en route. See Figure 2 and think that:

- A small percentage of what is said, say roughly 20%, produces most of what matters.
- A large percentage of what is said, say roughly 80%, produces a relatively small amount of what matters.

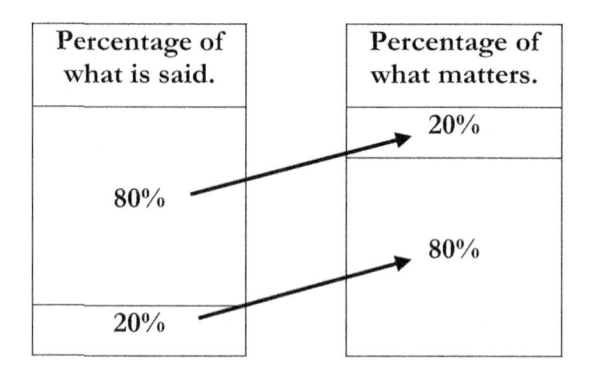

Figure 2. The 80:20 rule

Part of your job is to remove the rubbish and present the discussion as if it was short, logical and progressive, which it probably was not. Whatever shambles the meeting might have been, the minutes will make it look as if it was professional. Far better though if the meeting was professional in the first place.

For your notes, think of three categories of discussion happening at the meeting:

1	Much of the time.	General conversation and waffle. Filter out and reject much of it. Capture the meaningful pattern of the discussion.
2	Some of the time.	Key points. Zoom in. Get the meaning of what was said, not necessarily the actual words.
3	Occasionally.	Summaries, decisions, proposals (or 'motions' if very formal), proposer and seconder, votes, objections, etc. Record the actual words as best as you can, almost verbatim.

Once again, you can see here the immense value of a chair giving good summaries – and speaking slowly enough for you to write them down accurately.

Here, with some repetitions, are some ideas that people have found helpful:
1. Sit next to the chair, your partner. You can see and hear everyone and you can whisper or pass notes to the chair (such as asking for

clarification or a summary).
2. Have a comfortable chair.
3. Use a signature sheet: print the members names on a sheet of paper and get them to sign in. Not only does it give you the 'Present' list for your minutes but you know who to chase afterwards if you need to clarify any issues.
4. If you do not know all the people there, make a little map of where people are sitting.
5. Use a large pad rather than a secretary's notepad, although this is really a question of personal preference.
6. Use the table as a good supporting surface.
7. Practise using the Cornell method for taking notes, which is described in the next chapter.
8. When you get lost (as we all do), pick up again as soon as you can and abandon what was lost. Leave a large space of a about two inches or five centimetres, or more, but record the initials of the speaker. Later, check with them or the chair.
9. Ask for assistance with getting an accurate record of the decisions taken and the names of proposers, seconders, summaries, etc. If appropriate for the meeting, read out to the group what you have noted for these vital bits so they can correct you if you have made a mistake. This is a professional approach so do not be frightened of doing it but check with the chair if it is an appropriate thing to do for that particular meeting. Many minute takers worry that this seems to show a lack of confidence or ability on their part. Instead, see it as a professional technique for checking at source.
10. Do not rely on making an audio recording of the meeting. Microphones pick up lots of extraneous noises, even someone tapping on the other end of the table. In some rooms you almost need a professional system wired in to be certain of capturing everyone clearly. Anyway, do you really have time to listen to it all later? Do you really want to wade through a long recording to find the bit you missed? For some people having an audio recording of the meeting is a helpful reassurance. Ok! But never rely on it. If you do record the meeting, be sure to inform visitors that you are doing so just in case they object – and write the times when new items start so you have a reasonable chance of finding the right bit on the recording.

Yet again, the most important point of all: make sure the chair remembers to summarise so you can write down those jewels verbatim.

Many minute takers have asked me about using shorthand, or even if they should learn shorthand. Shorthand can be less useful that you might think as it is aimed primarily at taking dictation and taking dictation is the last thing you should be doing for most of the meeting. The time when shorthand is useful for a minute taker is for those occasions we have mentioned where you need to go verbatim – mostly when your dear chair gives one of his or her marvellous summaries or someone is making a proposal. But it is not worth the struggle of learning shorthand just for that.

However, develop your own 'shorthand' of abbreviations and acronyms as that can be useful, such as 'mgt' (management), 'mtg' (meeting), 'cmt' (committee), and so on.

If you are already good at shorthand, please do not use it to record everything being said. Remember, you are not taking dictation. You should be listening, filtering and being very selective, and you cannot do any of those things well if you are taking dictation. Limit your shorthand to getting those summaries and proposals down verbatim.

8

CORNELL NOTE-TAKING METHOD

The Cornell note-taking method is a good and recognised technique for taking notes. It was originally promoted for university or college students to take lecture notes. It is variously known as the Cornell Note Taking System, the Cornell Method or the Two-Column Method and is attributed to Professor Walter Pauk of Cornell University. (*How to Study in College*, first published in 1962.)

Although devised for taking notes of lectures, the Cornell Method can be used for any type of note taking, such as studying from a book – or taking notes for the minutes of a meeting.

The concept is simple yet powerful. Preferably with a full-size notepad (A4 or Letter), divide the page into two columns: make the left column about one third the width of the page and the right column about two thirds the width. Mark up as many pages as you think you will need for the meeting. (See Figure 3.)

About one-third the width	About two-thirds the width
Key words column	**Notes column**
Key points as bullets	Notes, notes, notes, notes, notes, notes, notes, notes, notes
	Notes, notes, notes, notes, notes, notes, notes
Key points as bullets	Notes, notes, notes, notes, notes, notes, notes

Minute Taking

	Notes, notes, notes, notes, notes
Key points as bullets	Notes, notes, notes, notes, notes, notes, notes, notes, notes (GF)
Key points as bullets	Notes, notes, notes, notes, notes, notes, notes, notes
Etc.	Etc.

Figure 3. The Cornell note-taking method

During the meeting, write your notes as usual in the right-hand column and leave the left column blank. Filter what you hear and try to keep your notes sensibly brief. Use very short sentences of around five to ten words – or ignore sentence structure altogether. Of course, write out the summaries, proposals and so on as verbatim as you can.

As soon as possible after the meeting (and your time management skills may be tested by this), review your notes and write the key points, key words and key phrases, key ideas and so on in the left column. Think bullet points! You can even paraphrase *brief* summaries in the left column. The very act of writing these bullets soon after the meeting will help your short-term memory to hang on to the meaning but, more importantly, we will use these bullet points (left-hand column) when we come to writing up the minutes.

Some people also like to make a small margin down the right edge of the page and put the speaker's initials there (not part of the Cornell Method). It can, however, be easier to write the initials as part of your notes and put a circle round them.

For minute taking, that is all there is to it. However, the full Cornell Method also saved a space of around five lines at the bottom of each page where the student could later write a summary of the information on that page, as an aid to thinking about what had been said and helping to memorise it. Also, there was a row at the top of the page for the title (you can use that, of course) and the page number.

The Cornell Method's secrets are to use only the wide column for your notes during the meeting, use short sentences (maybe ignoring punctuation issues) and, soon afterwards, to write key points in the narrow column. If coping with two columns on your notepad is not for you, then use the full width of your pad for your notes, with short sentences, and later capture the key message as bullet points elsewhere, maybe directly into your computer.

If you are a quick and accurate typist then you may prefer to write your notes directly into your computer. Later, add your key-points as bullets at the end of each minute – a sort of Cornell for the 21st century. We will want those bullet points when we write up the minutes.

9

I DO NOT UNDERSTAND WHAT THEY ARE TALKING ABOUT

So, you don't understand what they're talking about half the time? Really, for only half the time? Join the club!

It is quite normal for many minute takers, especially administrators, not to understand some, or even much, of what they hear. This is a near certainty when the committee members are specialists and the minute taker is not. The jargon might as well be a foreign language and it might feel like that sometimes. On the other hand, if you are a full member of the committee who also takes the minutes, then you will probably be familiar with it all.

You may feel a bit apprehensive about interrupting and asking for clarification but do it anyway. As we have said before, you may be helping others who are also struggling but do not want to risk looking foolish because they are supposed to understand. If you are not a subject specialist then of course you do not understand some of it. Nevertheless, whether you do or not, it is still your job to make an accurate record. So how do we solve this problem?

You know the answer by now. Back to our management team of two. During your pre-briefing with the chair be sure to explain this problem and ask the chair to provide those summaries. Remember, it is standard good practice for the chair to summarise at the end of each topic, but many do not. You may have to prompt them – and that is good practice on your part. As we mentioned earlier, occasionally the chair may ask someone else to summarise because they know the topic better.

Also, especially during long discussions, ask the chair for a summary at any sensible time, such as when you are lost or feel you have missed something important. Get these summaries down verbatim and you will have the core of your notes, even if you are still not sure what they mean.

Requesting summaries is one thing, but if you regularly minute such meetings then you have a professional duty to learn something about the most common topics that are discussed. Of course, you will not become a subject expert (if you do, ask for more pay) but you can probably pick up some of the basics and jargon.

Remember the most important lesson: Ask!

10

PRACTICE

The next point is personal: how good do you want to be?

The fact that you are reading this suggests that you do want to improve. You know the saying that practice makes perfect? Well, I'm not quite sure about that (I could practise singing for ever but still sound awful.) At least, practice normally leads to improvement.

Filtering the important from the less important is a crucial skill and it needs practice. Where better to practice filtering, or sifting the wheat from the chaff, and taking notes using the two-column approach, than at home where you can make as many mistakes as you wish and bin the lot afterwards? Well, you might think of many better places including at work where you are paid for the time – but at home is a good place.

Try it with radio or television programmes, especially those that have a mix of facts and opinions such as the news or documentaries. At first, forget about taking notes and just listen for the key points being made, separating the facts from the opinions. Do not even have a pen or pencil and paper to hand. If you record the programme, you can even check it afterwards to see how good you were if you really want to. You may be surprised at how many (informed) opinions there are amongst the facts and you will develop your skills at sifting one from the other.

Once you are happy that your listening skills are improving, take some notes using short sentences. Try the two-column method. Take your notes in the wide, right-hand column, keeping sentences short, and leaving the narrow, left-hand column blank. Wait for an hour or two and then capture the key points as bullets in the left-hand column. You can do this on paper or on a computer using its table facility (two columns and many rows).

If you prefer to use the full width of the paper or screen, then insert bullet points later at suitable points, maybe after a paragraph or two.

Practise your own abbreviations and acronyms of common expressions, a sort of personal shorthand, to help you to take notes quickly. When writing by hand, for instance, a plus sign or a small loop will serve for 'and'.

11

FROM NOTES TO MINUTES

For many minute takers, converting the notes into minutes is a laborious and time-gobbling process, often taking longer than the meeting itself. For committee members, delayed minutes are less useful than they could be. The very worst scenario is when minutes are issued at the start of the following meeting. What use are they then?

Issue the minutes as soon as you can, say two days for monthly meetings and next day for weekly ones. The longer the delay, the harder they are to write and the less useful they are. Such tight timescales are challenging but they are important. Plan your time so that you can achieve these timescales.

One lady told me that she was secretary for several managers who did not co-ordinate her time. Far too often, when she finished minuting one meeting she immediately went to minute another one, and then another one. She had a stack of notes waiting to be written up into minutes. Some were weeks old. She never had time to write up. She was stressed out and on the point of resigning. How did her managers allow such a thing to happen and why had she not said anything?

Tight timescales are daunting so, is there a faster way to write up good minutes? The good news is that, yes, there is. At first glance it might not seem faster but, with a bit of practice, it certainly is.

The secret is to break up the task of writing into three separate phases or stages and complete each one before starting the next.
1. Plan the minutes on your computer as a set of bullet points for each item or minute. Just copy the key points from the left column of your notes, adding or deleting information as appropriate. Turn them into bullet points and click and drag them into the most logical order. (Bear in mind that the speaker may have spoken with little preparation so the original sequence may be a bit haphazard.)
2. Expand the bullet points into sentences to get the draft minutes.

3. Edit the draft into the final minutes.

The fact is that most of us plan, write and edit our writing at the same time. Doing these three things simultaneously is not helpful and we end up rewriting much of it, maybe several times. We get into a muddle and it takes hours. Separating them sounds long-winded but it does save time in the end because it eliminates most of that 'muddle in the middle'. Many professional writers do this because it helps them to produce logical and well-written copy reasonably quickly. If it works for them then maybe it will work for us too.

Note that above I said 'draft', not 'first draft' and 'second draft' and so on because you may manage with only one draft. Having several drafts suggests that you have not done enough planning. OK, maybe that is a bit idealistic – but it is something to aim for and it can be achieved.

Stage one: Plan the minutes.

Discussions often wander around a lot. Meetings may even divert from one item to another and back again (for instance, when a visitor arrives and then leaves). Members can wax lyrical about their favourite topic, perhaps with increasing irrelevancy. When the chair fails to control this quickly with a 'mid-course correction', the meeting goes off track.

Despite your best efforts to filter, your notes will follow this muddled, meandering path to some extent, but your minutes should not. Fig. 4 pictures this meandering discussion and the final straight-to-the-point minutes.

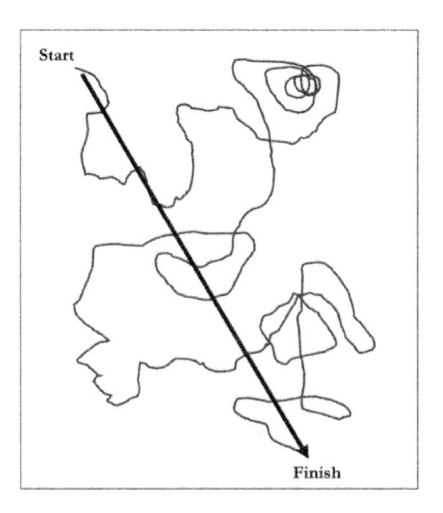

Figure 4. The discussion path versus the minutes path

From Notes to Minutes

Your job now is to sort out the wanderings and present the minutes in a logical order based on the agenda, cutting out the irrelevancies and presenting a 'straight line' discussion from start to finish. This is when your left-column bullet points take centre stage.

For each topic on the agenda, gather into one group all those bullet points of key words, phrases, ideas and so on from your notes.

Then, again for each individual agenda topic, rearrange the bullets into the most logical sequence, straightening out that meandering curve. Click and drag the bullets until they are all in their correct place. Maybe, add new ones from the right-hand column of your notes or delete any as you see fit.

You may have a lot of bullet points for each individual agenda topic. So, now split them up into sensible subgroups (embryo paragraphs), so that each bullet point (embryo sentence) belongs with its companions in one subgroup. Put the subgroups into a sensible order and put their bullet points into a sensible order. (See Fig. 5.)

Bullet the key points for each agenda item/minute.	Rearrange into a logical sequence, but a single group.	Make subgroups and arrange them and bullets logically.	
• Bullet A • Bullet B • Bullet C • Bullet D • Bullet E • Bullet F • Bullet G • Bullet H • Bullet I • Bullet J	• Bullet A • Bullet C • Bullet D • Bullet B • Bullet E • Bullet F • Bullet G • Bullet I • Bullet H • Bullet J	• Bullet A • Bullet C • Bullet D • Bullet B • Bullet E • Bullet F • Bullet G • Bullet I • Bullet H • Bullet J	Introduction Discussion Decision/ Action
Next minute.			

Figure 5. Using bullet points to sequence your paragraphs and sentences.

You now have a plan for each individual agenda topic: a group of bullet points split into subgroups, sensibly arranged, with their own bullet points, sensibly arranged. You are nearly there.

All the bullet points are embryo sentences arranged in the right sequence within their own subgroup. And the subgroups are embryo paragraphs lined up and waiting to spring into maturity as a complete minute.

As part of this planning, remember – introduction, discussion, decision and action (possibly combining the last two).

When you have done this for every agenda item, you have broken away from the actual sequence of the meeting and brought order to the sequence – and you have a plan for all your minutes. All that without thinking about paragraphs or sentences.

Stage two: Draft the minutes.

With such a detailed plan, writing the draft becomes relatively easy because now you only have to concentrate on putting sentences together and without even worrying much (yet) about the quality of the writing. That bit comes later in stage three when you edit the draft. For now, just write.

Concentrate on turning those bullet points into sentences. Sometimes, you may find that one bullet point needs two or even three sentences to bring out the meaning, that is fine. Equally, two bullet points may combine to give one sentence. Occasionally, you may decide to add an extra sentence directly from your notes in that earlier right-hand column. Let your plan guide you, very occasionally modifying it if necessary (no plan is perfect).

Importantly, at this drafting stage do not stop writing to try and find the perfect word. Keep the writing flow going and find the perfect word later when editing. That is, partly, what editing is for.

Eliminate interruptions and distractions. If possible, shut yourself away somewhere, away from the phone (silence it), email (turn off the alert), texts and visitors, so that you can concentrate on writing for a period of thirty or forty minutes or so. Interruptions are the writer's curse (except when you are ready for a break and a chat). This is concentrated work and can be quite tiring so you will probably need a short break after thirty or forty minutes.

Switch off the spell checker and the grammar checker too. That might seem odd and you will definitely want their help later of course, but right now they are just another source of interruptions. Do not worry (yet) if the English is not brilliant as you will improve it at the third stage (editing).

Stage three: Edit the draft minutes into the final version.

Editing is the final stage but it can still take quite a time depending on how good you are at writing great English at the first attempt. Most of us need to revise the draft at least once to get something we are happy with. So, now, call in the cavalry by turning on the spelling and grammar checkers.

Editing is about improving your raw diamond into a real gem. You do this in a similar way to a gem cutter, by cutting off the bits you do not want and polishing what is left. Many famous writers have commented on how much they cut out of their draft documents. Some say that the writer's motto is, 'Cut! Cut! Cut!' So, look for any repetitions and wordy sentences and deal with them. Cut!

At times you may not quite get the right word, so now is the time to check a dictionary or a thesaurus to find the word you really want. Use the spell checker, of course, to find typing mistakes but do not rely on it because, as you know, it cannot spot typos that result in a genuine, but wrong, word: such as 'work' instead of 'word' or 'if' instead of 'is'. And, as of course you know, be sure it is set to your version of English (such as UK or US).

Use the grammar checker as well. I have met many people who do not like the grammar checker in Microsoft Word. True, it can be irritating when it tells you something is wrong when it is right, but it is an extremely useful tool and is programmed with far more rules of grammar than most of us know (well over 150).

Delve below the surface of the grammar checker and you will find a built-in style checker. Change the setting (under 'Options') to 'grammar and refinements' as it will then look for more issues. I can almost guarantee that it will spot issues you have missed. Always, however, make your own decisions about anything the grammar and style checkers tell you.

After you have completed all this work on the computer, print the minutes and read them quietly and slowly. It is amazing what else you discover when you read your own writing on paper rather than on the screen. Also, try reading them very quickly (aloud, if possible, although that might not be practical). Reading quickly can flush out bits that do not quite flow satisfactorily.

Here are some other points that might be helpful, with a reminder of some of those we have just looked at.

- Only include a discussion if really necessary, then keep it short and to the point, cutting out unnecessary detail.
- Highlight action points.
- Keep paragraphs short, aiming for an average length of around four to six lines.
- Keep sentences short, aiming for an average length below about 18 words.
- Avoid long sentences. More than about 35 words may be getting difficult to read and will be harder for you to punctuate. A string of

long sentences demands a lot from readers (and you).
- Use plain English where you can, avoiding unnecessary jargon, but accepting that many minutes contain a lot of jargon appropriate to the committee.
- Be specific: for instance, 'Eastern Trains' rather than 'the train company'.
- Cut unnecessary adjectives and adverbs, such as 'value-added improvement'. 'Improvement' will probably do the job.
- Normally, slightly prefer the active voice (the sub-committee recommended...) to the passive voice (it was recommended by the sub-committee...). The grammar checker will flag such sentences with the statement, 'Saying who or what did the action would be clearer'.
- Slightly prefer verbs to nouns ('the chair has seen...' rather than 'the chair has had sight of...'; 'the Committee decided ...' rather than 'the Committee made a decision...').
- Check all grammar, spelling and punctuation.
- Make it look good – it encourages people to read.
- Print your minutes and read them. Fix any obvious problems.

APPENDIX A – DIFFERENT STYLES

It is worth having a look at an example of each of the three types of minutes we described earlier, verbatim, discussion and action. Although fictional, they show the basic differences. However, do remember that there are not really three styles but a whole range of them that move slowly from verbatim to discussion to action depending on how much discussion there is.

Have a look at each 'style' and see what you like and dislike about each one. Think about why you like or dislike it and which one is the closest to what you already do and what you think you will aim to do in the future.

Near-verbatim minutes

New Catering Contract

The committee discussed the tenders received. JK (House Services) reminded the committee that invitations to tender for the new catering contract, which is due to start on 1 January, were sent to five companies early in October, including to the existing contractor, Alpha Foods. The other four were: Beta, Gamma, Delta and Epsilon. This was agreed unanimously back in the September meeting.

JK suggested eliminating two of the bids: Beta Foods because their bid did not meet the minimum requirements for choice of food and drinks (they were way short), and Gamma Foods because their bid was almost twice the price of most of the others (specifically about 70% more expensive). This was agreed unanimously.

Although not the cheapest, JK recommended Alpha Foods because they have established a consistently good track record with us over the past three years and have incorporated into their bid all of the suggestions we have made to them for improvements.

LG (Finance) observed that cost is always of great importance and that every pound saved is a pound on the bottom line. Although Alpha Foods were not the lowest bidder, the difference between them and the lowest bidder was quite small. JK pointed out that whilst Delta Foods is the lowest bidder, they have received recent public criticism over their hygiene standards. This occurred since the invitations to tender were sent out so we were not aware of this at the time. She had not yet been able to verify the details and was quoting from a report in a local newspaper.

BN (Marketing) felt it was unwise to be seen to endorse publicly a company that might be at risk of a food hygiene infringement. He said that Epsilon Foods have a good reputation and are well known for their sponsorship of the local football club, which might have knock-on marketing benefits to us. LG commented that at the prices they were charging they could sponsor two football clubs and that football sponsorship was not a good reason to choose such a high bid.

After further discussion, the committee decided to accept the bid from Alpha Foods, subject to them making the improvements itemised in their bid, with a starting date of the 1 January. This was proposed by JK, seconded by LG and agreed unanimously. AM was asked to inform Alpha Foods and arrange for their current Catering Manager to visit for discussion with JK on how the proposed improvements are to be implemented, and to thank the other four bidders for their bids and inform them that they were unsuccessful on this occasion.

Action: AM by 3 Nov.

With 432 words this includes a lot of detail and much of it may not be needed. Even so, the actual conversation would have had far more words so it is not really verbatim in the strict sense of that word. Keep asking yourself how much detail is needed. The answer will depend on the committee and especially on the purpose of the minutes.

Discussion or Summary minutes

New Catering Contract

The committee discussed the tenders received from five bidders for the new catering contract, which is due to start on 1 January. In October, five bidders were invited to tender: Alpha, Beta, Gamma, Delta and Epsilon.

Alpha Foods, the existing contractor, has a good track record with us and has incorporated into its bid all of the suggestions we made for improvements. Beta Foods did not meet the minimum requirements for choice of food and drinks. The bids from Gamma and Epsilon were much higher than the other bids. Delta Foods have had recent bad publicity over hygiene matters.

It was decided to accept the bid from Alpha Foods, subject to the improvements already agreed, and to thank the other bidders for their bids and inform them that they were unsuccessful on this occasion. AM to action and invite Alpha's Catering Manager to visit to discuss with JK how to implement the improvements listed in their bid. Proposed by JK, seconded by LG and agreed unanimously.

Action: AM by 3 Nov.

At 166 words, this version is far less than half the length of the previous one but it includes all the essentials. The first paragraph gives the introduction, the second covers the discussion and the third merges the decision and action into one paragraph.

Decision/Action minutes

New Catering Contract
Five tenders were received. Alpha Foods Ltd's bid (the existing contractor) was accepted. AM to inform them giving a start date of 1 January, subject to the improvements already agreed, and invite their Catering Manager to visit to discuss with JK the implementation of the improvements. AM to thank the others and inform them that their bids were unsuccessful.

Action: AM by 3 Nov.

This cuts out the introduction and discussion, and it delivers the decision and action including the deadline in 59 words. It could be shorter; the following version has 45 words:

Resolved to award the new contract to Alpha Foods Ltd starting 1 January, subject to the improvements already agreed, to inform them and to invite their Catering Manager to visit to discuss with JK the implementation of the improvements, and to thank the other bidders.

Action: AM by 3 Nov.

If the action point was written in the objective style, it would have been something like this. It is an instruction and includes the fact that the information should be in writing. It has 59 words.

AM to write to Alpha Foods to inform them that their bid is accepted and to arrange for their Catering Manager to visit to discuss with JK how to implement the improvements. Also, to write to the other four bidders to thank them for their bids and inform them that they were unsuccessful on this occasion. Deadline: 3 Nov.

As you can see, at 432 words the near-verbatim version is long-winded. Whilst the information is correct, much of it is not needed. Sadly, it is typical of too many minutes where the minute taker has laboured long and hard only for the users to find them too boring to read. Who wants, let alone needs, all that detail? Well, in fact, some may!

As we said much earlier, minutes must be fair to all parties. Sometimes that means that additional details are needed, especially in cases where you should show that some issues, ideas, concerns, etc. were thoughtfully considered but were overridden in the final decision.

By comparison, the Action Minutes are very short, with the second version only having 45 words.

Even shorter action minutes might look like these:

By 3 Nov, AM to inform Alpha Foods Ltd that their bid was successful and invite their Catering Manger to discuss the improvements with JK. And to inform the others that they were not successful and to thank them. (39 words)

By 3 Nov, AM to thank and inform all bidders of the outcome for them and invite Alpha Foods Ltd to discuss with JK the implementation of the improvements. (29 words)

The last version poses the risk that AM might miss the 'for them' and tell everyone who made the winning bid. This might be pushing conciseness for the sake of it a bit too far – take care, there are no prizes for the fewest words.

Conciseness is good and when editing, you can always play around with the wording of your minutes to see what you can delete, bearing in mind that you need to issue the minutes quickly. Realistically, other work gets in the way but it is worth devoting a little time to seeing what you can cut out.

The discussion or summary minutes are the most common type. The sample above has 166 words and, while it could be a little shorter, it does the job without too much effort. As stated earlier, there is no one size fits all and discussion minutes fill the great range between verbatim and action minutes. You try to give as much detail as your committee really needs and no more, which (as we have said before) may well be considerably less than you – and they – think they want.

APPENDIX B – RESPONSIBILITIES

Here are some ideas about how responsibilities are shared between you and the chair. They will not all apply to you but note the ones that do. Possibly there are other things your organisation expects you to do as well.

Before the meeting

CHAIR

- Define the meeting's purpose.
- Read previous minutes.
- Define the agenda, tell or consult the minute taker.
- Decide who should attend.
- Decide any important seating arrangements including the minute taker being next to you.
- Brief the minute taker and provide any help needed.
- Check the organisation's Quality Procedures for holding meetings.
- Prepare self.

MINUTE TAKER

- Check the meeting's purpose.
- Read previous minutes.
- Record any corrections to previous minutes.
- Meet the chair, request summaries, clarify any issues including how best to communicate with each other.
- Prepare, agree and distribute agenda.
- Ensure that any documents are distributed early.
- List action points for matters arising.
- Check/book room, equipment, refreshments, etc.
- Record apologies as you receive them.
- Prepare an attendance list for signatures.
- Prepare self.

During the meeting

CHAIR

- Arrive early.
- Start and end on time.
- Is there a quorum?
- Introduce people, minute taker and topics.
- Define the meeting rules. One speaker at a time, stick to the point, no private conversations.
- Agree/sign previous minutes.
- Control the meeting, keep order, keep to time.
- Help minute taker.
- Encourage or restrain members as appropriate.
- Summarise periodically, especially after decisions and at end of each topic.

MINUTE TAKER

- Arrive early.
- Take spare copies of papers and pens – for others.
- Take reference files, if any.
- Have previous minutes ready for the chair to sign.
- Have attendance list for signatures.
- Check room, temperature, noise, etc.
- Sit next to the chair.
- Is there a quorum?
- Listen carefully, taking notes.
- Be selective, filter.
- Check your understanding. Ask questions if stuck.
- Ask for summaries.
- Clarify decisions or anything you are not clear about.

After the meeting

CHAIR

- Clarify issues for the minute taker as necessary.
- Check and correct/approve the draft minutes within one day of receiving them.
- Check and monitor that action points are taking place (often delegated to minute taker).
- Prepare for next meeting.

MINUTE TAKER

- Clear room; especially remove any spare confidential papers.
- Clarify difficult points with the chair or others.
- Send papers issued at the meeting to absentees.
- Agree the draft minutes with the chair within 1 or 2 days.
- Issue approved minutes within 2 or 3 days.
- Follow-up action points for the chair if asked to do so.
- Prepare for next meeting.

APPENDIX C – A SHORT GUIDE TO EDITING

Remember the three stages: planning, drafting and editing. Keep them separate and do not edit while you are writing the draft. Editing is the process of turning your draft set of minutes into the final, polished version. There will always be ways to improve your draft minutes so you must always edit them. Here are some thoughts to help you with your editing.

Spelling
- Use the spell checker but do not rely on it. It will miss words that have been misspelt only to produce a real, but wrong, word (e.g. work/word, live/lice, dine/vine, if/is/it/in, naval/navel, vest/west and so on).
- Check that it is set to the correct version of English (Tools/Language).
- Also, have a good dictionary available as a standard reference for spelling.

Paragraphs
- Check that paragraphs are arranged in a logical sequence.
- Check the length of paragraphs and keep most of them under about six lines. Short paragraphs are easier to understand than long ones, so cut long paragraphs in two.
- Start with a strong sentence that leads into the paragraph. Grab the reader's attention right at the start. *AK proposed that...*
- Start a new paragraph when you start a new subject.
- Leave a line between paragraphs to improve the appearance.

Sentences
- Short sentences are easier to understand than long ones.

- Aim for an average length of up to about 18 words.
- Split very long sentences, say those over about 35words.
- If you have to use a very long sentence, try to make the next sentence especially short.
- Aim for simple punctuation – its purpose is to help the reader to understand, not to please professors of English grammar.

Words
- Use the specialist words the committee members use, which will include their professional jargon. Other than that, prefer plain English whenever you can.
- Otherwise, short words are often easier to understand than long ones and are usually understood by more people.
- The English language is very rich in its variety of words, there are always alternatives to cumbersome (*awkward*) or grandiose (*showy*) words.

Superfluous words

Avoid superfluous words, usually adjectives and adverbs. In meetings, people speak as they think and may rely on casual, almost colloquial, phrases. Do not put them in the minutes. Here are a few examples, you will know many more:
- a serious crisis
- real danger
- active consideration
- few in number
- brief in duration
- one and the same
- part and parcel of
- plan in advance
- shuttle back and forth
- irreducible minimum.

Clichés

Clichés are apt phrases that have become boring through overuse. People will use clichés during the meeting but leave them out of the minutes. Here are a few examples, you will know many more:
- take the bull by the horns
- conspicuous by its absence
- raring to go

- at this moment in time
- touch base later
- take this off-line
- square the circle
- singing from the same hymn sheet
- level playing field
- reinvent the wheel.

Active and passive voices
The grammar checker in MS Word is good at identifying passive sentences (such as, *the mat was sat on by the cat*) and gives the message 'saying who or what did the action would be clearer'. The alternative active sentence (*the cat sat on the mat*) is preferred because it is also usually shorter.
Examples:

• It was recommended by the sub-committee...	Passive
• The sub-committee recommended...	Active
• Both buildings were visited by the inspectors.	Passive
• The inspectors visited both buildings.	Active
• Staff are encouraged by managers to try new ideas.	Passive
• Managers encourage staff to try new ideas.	Active

Verbs instead of nouns
Sometimes using a verb instead of a noun can shorten a sentence.

Noun	**Verb**
• *The union is making a recommendation...*	• *The union recommends...*
• *The committee took into consideration...*	• *The committee considered...*
• *IT conducted an evaluation of...*	• *IT evaluated...*
• *The consultants have made an analysis of...*	• *The consultants analysed...*
• *Staff made an arrangement to...*	• *Staff arranged to...*

Many of these nouns end in ...*ment*, or ...*tion* or ...*ion*. The equivalent verbs are likely to end in ...*ing* or ...*ed*, or have *to* in front.

Sexist language
There are two main problem areas: gender-specific words and personal pronouns.
Gender-specific
Some words change to indicate the gender of the individual, such as *waiter*

and *waitress*; others do not, such as *teacher, driver* and *writer*. Avoid sexist language if you can do so without spoiling the structure. For example, you could use *chairperson* or *chair* instead of *chairman, supervisor* instead of *foreman*, etc.

Personal pronouns: he, she, it

In English we do not use *it* as a pronoun for people. Using *he or she, his and hers* and *him and her* can become cumbersome. When writing about general issues, it may be better to use the plural: *they, theirs, them.*

Example:

- *A secretary should take responsibility for her minutes.* Sexist.
- *A secretary should take responsibility for his or her minutes.* Not sexist, but a bit cumbersome.
- *Secretaries should take responsibility for their minutes.* Not sexist.

Readability statistics

MS Word can measure some statistics to help you judge how readable your document is. You can access these in the Editor under 'Insights, Document stats'. (In older versions of Word you need to switch them on by clicking: *Tools, Options, Spelling & Grammar* and selecting *Show Readability Statistics*. They are then displayed after a spell check.) The most useful statistics are the average sentence length, the percentage of sentences that are passive, and the number of words.

APPENDIX D – PUNCTUATION

This short guide is based on the Style Guide in The Concise Oxford Dictionary and the Chicago Manual of Style.

Apostrophe
- Use in contractions to show where a letter has been omitted: *wasn't, can't*. (Only use contractions in minutes that are very informal.)
- Use to denote the possessive: *Sally's, the boss's*.
    - Apostrophe before the *s* in singulars and irregular plurals: *Sally's responsibility, the boy's family*, one boy), *the women's meeting*; similarly with time, *one week's delay*.
    - Apostrophe after the *s* in regular plurals: *the boys' families* (more than one boy), *the babies' check-ups*; similarly with time, *two weeks' delay*.
    - Be consistent with names ending with *s*: either *James' report* or *James's report*. Both are acceptable.
- Use an apostrophe in *its* only if a letter is missing. *It's a crying shame…*, meaning *it is a crying shame*. Prefer to spell out in full in minutes. *Its* as a possessive has no apostrophe, just the same as *his, hers, ours, yours* and *theirs*.

Brackets
- Use to enclose additional information or asides: *In all cases (except where an exemption certificate has been issued and is in date)*.
- Use instead of two commas (where you want more emphasis).
- Use for citations, references and for spelling out abbreviations. *(See the attached report.)*

Capital letters
- Use to start a sentence, even a sentence in quotation marks within another sentence, and for proper names: *I told him, 'No!'. Peter Smith, British, American, the Government, Northern Ireland* (but *northern Scotland,*

- *northern England* as they are not political areas).
- Most trade names or trademarks (such as *BBC, IBM, Honda*) but not when the name has become generic such as *biro*.
- Titles: *Vice-President, Dr, Mr, Mrs, Ms, etc.*
- Personal pronoun: *I*.
- First and main words in a title: *Proposal and Budgetary Quotation for removing Asbestos*.

Colon
- Use to introduce lists, including bullet points.
- Keep sentences short and you will probably not need colons.

Comma
- Too many commas become a distraction and too few can cause confusion.
- Use between two or more adjectives if the adjectives could be satisfactorily rearranged: *A small, light, complex piece of equipment*.
- Use in pairs as if they are brackets: *The bike, which was expensive, was broken*.
- Use to separate items in a simple list: *The chair visited Alpha, Beta, Gamma and Delta* (British style). American style tends to use a comma before the last item: *Alpha, Beta, Gamma, and Delta*.
- Use to separate numbers into thousands, etc. In some writing styles, spaces are used instead: *23,000* or *23 000*. A separator is not required with four-digit numbers: *3500*.

Dash
If using the 'en dash', which tends to be preferred in British writing:
- Use in pairs – instead of two commas – where extra emphasis is needed.
- Use to indicate a pause – for emphasis.

If using the 'em' dash, which tends to be preferred in American writing:
- Use in pairs—instead of two commas—where extra emphasis is needed.
- Use to indicate a pause—for emphasis.

Exclamation mark
- Use after an exclamation, whether a word or phrase: *Stop!* Exclamation remarks are rare in minutes.

Full stop
- Use at the end of a sentence.
- Usually omitted in common abbreviations, especially in correspondence: *Mr P Smith, BBC (not B.B.C.), IBM (not I.B.M.).*

Hyphen
- Use to join two words together: *start-up,* but *nationwide.* Check in a dictionary to be sure as there can appear to be little logic in deciding which terms are single words, which are hyphenated and which remain as two words.
- Use to link two or more adjectives before a noun, especially if the meaning needs to be made clear to the reader: *a twentieth-century problem* (but *a problem of the twentieth century*), *English-speaking people.*

Period. See 'Full stop'

Question mark
- Do not use if the question is merely implied, not stated.

Quotation marks
- Use to indicate direct speech, or quotations or quoted words.
- On rare occasions you may need to include a quotation in minutes, most likely from a document rather than from speech. Place punctuation marks belonging to the quotation inside the main quotation marks, those belonging to the larger sentence go outside: *'Did the previous instructions say, "Danger!"?'* Note the single and double quotation marks. Some organisations prefer to use them the other way round: *"Did the previous instructions say, 'Danger!'?"* Whichever approach you choose, use it consistently. (All of this will confuse many software grammar checkers.)
- Do not use quotation marks merely because you cannot think of the right word: *At this stage of the investigation GR also 'touched base' with other departments.* Instead, say precisely what GR did, such as *spoke with, wrote to,* etc.

Semicolon
- While normally you use commas to separate items in a list, if the items are complicated then they may need commas themselves. In such cases, use colons to separate the items.
- Use to unite two sentences into one. *There is minimum technical risk; there is some financial risk.* (It may be better to have two sentences or use a conjunction such as *and, but.*)
- Not often now used at the end of bullet points.

APPENDIX E – SUMMARY

Purpose
- Every meeting should have a purpose, what is the purpose of your meeting? Check with the chair if you are not sure.
- All minutes have a purpose. This is to provide an official and neutral record of the important decisions made at the meeting and their action points with, usually, a brief description of how those decisions were reached.
- Other useful information is included, such as who attended, etc.

Agenda
- Issue the agenda far enough in advance to allow everyone time to prepare and, if necessary, ask for items to be added. The chair decides whether to add them or not.
- For a few and very informal meetings, the agenda could simply be a list on a flip chart or screen.
- Give a start time for the meeting and, ideally, a finish time.
- Clarify whether each agenda item is for information, discussion or decision.
- Put the most important items high on the agenda.

Preparation
- Have a talk with the chair before the meeting.
- Ask the chair to summarise regularly and at the end of each agenda item (standard good practice).
- Read the previous minutes.
- Learn more about the regular topics.
- Prepare the room.
- Practice note taking using the Cornell or two-column method.

At the meeting
- Sit next to the chair.
- Check that there is a quorum, i.e. the minimum number of members present for the meeting to proceed.
- Use the Cornell or two-column method.
- Write less, be selective, do more listening than writing.
- Ask for summaries.
- Record summaries, proposals (or motions if the meeting is very formal), decisions, actions, etc. verbatim.
- Use A4 or letter paper on a good writing surface.

After the meeting
- Clarify any issues you are not sure about with the chair or with other people.
- Draft the minutes the same day or the next day for discussion with the chair.
- Find a quiet place to write up and ensure you are free from interruptions for 30-40 minutes at a time.
- Use the left-hand column bullet points to plan your draft minutes.
- Turn off the spelling and grammar checkers while writing but turn them back on for editing.
- Keep the tasks of planning, drafting and editing separate.
- Issue the minutes within two or three days.

Minutes
- Agree a format for the minutes and if/how to number them.
- Keep them as simple as possible.
- Plan each minute using Introduction, Discussion, Decision/Action.
- Only use lengthy discussion minutes if you really have to.
- 'Present' – members at the meeting; 'apologies' – those who sent their apologies, 'in attendance' – visitors. Some chairs will use 'absent' to name and shame. 'Observers' – for example, members of the public, press or other media.
- Record those who were there for only part of the time.
- Sequence the minutes as listed in the agenda, regardless of what actually happened at the meeting.
- 'Committee business' refers to anything about the committee itself rather than the business being discussed.
- The minutes of the previous meeting must be approved. Record any corrections.
- 'Matters arising' is only for issues arising from the previous meeting or meetings.

- Make action points clear either by writing them on a new line, in bold and aligned right, or by putting them in a separate column to the right.

Taking notes and writing up
- Sit next to the chair.
- Listen carefully and filter out much of what is said. Remember the 80:20 rule, a lot of what is said does not need to be recorded. Get the essentials.
- Ask for summaries when you are struggling, when you simply do not understand what they are talking about, when decisions are made and at the end of each item.
- Use the Cornell method or adapt it to something that you are comfortable with.
- If you use shorthand, do not try to record everything because that means you have a lot to sort out later. Filter now!
- Rearrange the material to match the agenda sequence if the meeting diverted from the agenda sequence.
- Plan using bullet points for the items you want in the minutes.
- Arrange the bullet points into a logical order to provide embryo paragraphs and sentences for each agenda item.
- Convert them to sentences.
- Edit into the final version.
- Keep planning, writing and editing separate.

Minute Taking

APPENDIX F – SAMPLE MINUTES

Here is an example of the organisation of some fairly standard minutes. Note that the left-hand column records the number of each item as the year in two digits and the item number in sequence through the year. This makes it easy to refer to individual items in any set of minutes.

Minutes

**Weekly meeting of the Standing Committee
Monday 15 January 2024
in the Boardroom**

The meeting opened at 2.00 p.m.

Present:
Joan Pinnacle	Chair and MD
Frank Davies	Finance Director
Joanna Marsden	HR Director
Mary Jacobs	Marketing and Sales Director
Simon Wilson	Secretary

In attendance:
Noel Fielding, 24/05 only

Apologies:
Andrew Bosch, Manufacturing Manager

		Action
24/01	The minutes of the previous meeting, 8 Jan 2024, were approved.	

24/02 **Merger with Cunningham Composites**

The meeting received the report, presented by JP and circulated the previous week. JP outlined the main advantages and disadvantages of a merger. She stressed that Cunningham Composites (CC) had made the first approach and that she had concerns about their profitability.

FD was concerned that CC appear to be struggling. Their latest annual report shows a loss of about £2m, 20% worse than the previous year, and there are some large unsecured bank loans partially disguised in the annual report. Also, the pension fund is underfunded with an as yet unknown deficit.

FD to obtain clarification from the Finance Director of CC and prepare a one-page summary for next week's meeting. — **FD, by 22 Jan**

JM expressed concerns about overstaffing and high salaries. CC's ratio of headcount to turnover is 1.3 times that at Pinnacle and several functional sections have a higher staffing level than seems necessary, much higher than at Pinnacle. Salary levels are 15% higher for equivalent positions.

JP expressed concerns about the different organisational structure at CC. Although CC is approximately the same size as Pinnacle and has a similar number of sites around the country (seven and nine respectively), CC is regionally based whereas Pinnacle is functionally based. If merged, CC's functional structure would need to change, which would not be easy and would probably lead to redundancies and subsequent costs.

JP to investigate this further and report back to the next meeting. — **JP by 22 Jan**

Appendix F – Sample Minutes

24/03	**Burglary, 31 Dec 2023**	
	JP reported that there was a break in on the 31 Dec and three laptops were stolen. Police have arrested two people and recovered all three machines, although one is damaged beyond repair. Initial reports suggest that the strong passwords prevented the data from being accessed. The police are retaining the machines for now. All the data is backed up on the server.	
24/04	**Mary Jacobs retirement**	
	MJ will retire in six months' time and there are no suitable internal candidates to replace her. Agreed to look externally, aiming for a two-week handover from 1 July. Proposed by JP, seconded by FD and agreed unanimously.	
	JM to engage Angel Recruitment to look for suitable candidates.	**JM by 22 Jan**
24/05	**Buildings Refurbishment**	
	Noel Fielding (Site Manager) joined the meeting.	
	NF updated the committee on progress. Plans are now agreed with the architect and we are ready to ask them to go out to tender.	
	NF to ask the architects to prepare an invitation to tender and for him to bring it to the committee asap.	**NF by 16 Jan**
	Proposed by FD, seconded by JM, and agreed by all. JP thanked Noel for all the hard work he had put into this project which had proved more difficult than originally expected.
NF left the meeting.	
Etc.		

ABOUT THE AUTHOR

Tony Atherton is a retired trainer and not-yet-retired writer. After graduating with a degree in electronics and a PhD, he worked in the electrical and electronics industry for nearly 30 years.

This included time in the Royal Navy, with GEC-Marconi, as a lecturer at the University of Hong Kong, with the UK's Independent Broadcasting Authority, and as the training manager at NTL – now part of Virgin Media. He became a freelance trainer and writer in 1997.

For 25 years, Tony ran training courses for professional people in a wide variety of organisations. His most popular courses were report writing and minute taking. He has trained delegates at many public and private organisations in the UK and some in Europe.

He has written nearly a hundred articles for various magazines and has had seven books published, either by traditional publishers or Amazon.

BOOKS BY THIS AUTHOR

Technical Report Writing and Style Guide
Based around a long-running training course, it focusses on writing technical and engineering reports. The paperback and ebook versions are available on Amazon and Kindle.

Business Report Writing with Sample Report and Style Guide
Also based around a long-running training course, this is the sister book to the *Technical Report Writing* book. It is widely applicable to any type of business report. The paperback and ebook versions are available on Amazon and Kindle.

Report Writing for Professionals with Sample Report and Style Guide
Very similar to *Business Report Writing* but aimed at a wider audience and so applicable to anyone writing any type of report. The paperback and ebook versions are available on Amazon and Kindle.

30 Minutes Career Fast Track Kit - Market Yourself
This unique pack contains four best-selling titles from Kogan Page's popular 30 Minutes series that together represent the complete guide to achieving career success. Tony wrote one of the four books: *30 Minutes to Market Yourself*. Published by Kogan Page.

30 Minutes to Manage your Time Better
There are 168 hours in every week but some weeks it feels as if we have been short-changed. Where did the time go? This book advocates spending a few minutes each day taking control of your time. Published by Kogan Page.

How to be Better at Delegation and Coaching
Delegation and coaching are skills that complement each other. The book provides hints and tips on developing these skills to improve performance in organisations. It covers the processes involved in good delegation and

coaching and provides an action list of how to improve both skills. Published by Kogan Page.

From Compass to Computer: A History of Electrical and Electronics Engineering.

Although the history is well known to historians of science and technology it is relatively unknown to most practising engineers. This book brings them a readable account of how their subject developed from its early days as the two primitive sciences of electricity and magnetism to today's vast engineering applications. Published by Macmillan and San Francisco Press.

INDEX

Absent 6, **23**, 34, **38**, 78
Action 8-9, 30, 34-5, 39, 60, 62-5, 82
Action minutes 7, 9, **10-1**, **65-6**
Action points 6, 8-9, 12, 14, 20, 24, 34, **39**, 61, 68, 77, 79
Admin business 23, 38
Any other business, AOB 22, **26**, 27-30, **35**
Apologies 14, 16, **22-3**, 27-9, 34, **37-8**, 67, 78, 81
Approval of previous minutes 22, **23-4**, 28, 30, **38**
Approved 18, 24-5, 34-5, 39, 68, 78, 82
Attendance sheet: 17, 19, 47, 67-8
Attributable 10, **12**
Brainstorming 7, 44
Clarify 9, 15, **19**-20, 47, 67-8, 77-8
Committee business 22, **23**, 27-8, 30, 34, **38**, 78
Cornell method 47, **49-51**, 77, 78-9
Corrections 14, 16, 20, **23-4**, **38-9**, 67, 78
Date(s) 22-4, **26-7**, 29-30, 35, 40
Decision(s) 3, 6-12, 14, 24, 29-31, 34-6, 40, 46-7, 60-2, 65, 68, 77-9
Design the minutes 5, **7**
Discussion minutes 7-10, **11**, 58, **64**, 66, 78
Draft minutes 20-1, 57-8, **60-1**, 68-9, 78
Edit(ed/ing) 24, 58, **60-2**, 66, 69ff, 78-9
Estimated times 31
In attendance 33, 36, **37**, 78, 81

Introduction 7-10, 22-**3**, 60, 64-5, 78
Main agenda items 22, 24-**5**, 29, 36, 39
Matters arising **14**-6, 22, **24-5**, 27-30, **39**, 67, 78
Meet the chair **15**, 17, 43, 53, 67, 77
Number (s) (ing) 24-5, 28-9, **35-6**, 38, 45, 72, 78, 81
Objective style **9**, **29-30**, 31, 40, 65
Observers 34, **38**, 78
Part-time attendance 37
Plan (ning) 15, 19, 43, 57, 69, 78-9
Plan the minutes 58ff, 79
Present 3, 6, 18, 33, **36-8**, 78, 81
Press 5-6, 34, 78
Pronouns **36**, 71-2, 74
Public 5-6, 34, 38, 78
Purpose 5, 8-9, 14, 22-3, 25, 28, 34, **37**, 64, 67, 70, 77
Question 5-8, 11, **18-9**, 25, 68, 75
Quorum 18, 68, 78
Readability statistics 72
Reports 16-7, 22, **25**-6, 27-8, 30-1, 34
Retain minutes 26, 36
Sexist language 71-2
Signature, electronic 24
Signature sheet 17, 19, 47, 67-8
Substitutions 39
Summary (ies/ise) 7, 10-**1**, **15**-7, 19-20, 25, 42-4, 46-8, 50, 53-4, 64, 66-8, 78-9
Summary minutes **11**, **64**, 66
Time 13-6, 21-3, 25-6, **27**, 28, **31**, 38, 41, 44, 46-8, 57-8, 60, 66, 68, 73, 77-8

Title 7-8, 22, 25-6, 33, 37, 50, 74
Title block **22-3**, 26, 33
Verbatim **9-12**, 15, **19**, 46-48, 50, 54, **63**-4, 66, 78
Verbs 36, 62, 71
Welcome **22-3**, 27-30, 34, 36

Sample
Business Report Writing and Style Guide

CHAPTER 1 – LAYING THE FOUNDATIONS

How are reports like machines? Machines are designed for a defined purpose, then made and tested – they must do something and do it effectively and efficiently. So too with reports. They too must do something and do it effectively and efficiently. Often, they should convince or persuade someone to take some recommended action. As with machines, and other products, they should be designed, then made and then tested. Or in writing terms: planned, written, and edited.

How might we define a 'report'? A report should be a clear and concise account of an investigation, or part of an investigation, and its outcome. That account is very important to some people and is likely to guide decisions they have to make. They have asked a question and they want an answer. Notice the phrase, clear and concise – two vital qualities of good reports. So vital that we have already mentioned them twice.

Reports are also individual or stand-alone documents. In other words, the intended readers should not need to refer to other information to understand them. Of course, some reports are also part of a series such as monthly reports, and interim and final reports.

As I have hinted, a report is your product and many organisations (especially consultancies) 'manufacture' reports. Whether it is your personal work, which your managers will rely on, or a part of your organisation's work, which a client will rely on, your reports affect your reputation and that of your organisation. They create an impression in the minds of clients, suppliers, the public, the media and anyone else who reads them, and that can include your manager, senior managers and board members. A good report might help to build client loyalty; a bad report will damage it. Perhaps it is an exaggeration to say that a good report can enhance your career, but maybe a bad one can damage it for a while.

1.1 – Three Principles

What makes a good report? Many things help to make a report good but there are three big principles to note. The first is that the readers can see quickly that its specialist sections are robust, which helps them to trust it. The second is that the readers can follow the reasoning easily, which comes from a logical arrangement of, or sequence to, the information – logical that is to the readers. That also builds trust. The third is that the intended readers can understand it easily. That requires good, but not necessarily perfect, English.

Notice that all three principles focus on your readers' experience, not yours. My apologies, but your readers are the most important people here.

The first of the three principles, that the specialist parts are robust, lies outside the scope of this book. I trust your judgement on that score and have taken it as given. Being robust is one thing but convincing your readers that it is robust is something else. Convincing them starts with the aim of the report and it builds as you describe your methods, but more of that later.

The second principle is to sequence your information logically, in a way that your readers can relate to, so that they can follow it – instinctively. That starts by using the standard sections or format that your readers expect to see, which usually are the executive summary, introduction, findings (a word you may not use), analysis, discussion, conclusions and recommendations. We examine these in detail in Chapter 2. It is likely that your organisation's templates will dictate these, or a variation on them. A report is not the place for experimental arrangements although there are other formats, such as the managerial format or the 1:3:25 format – both of which we will look at later.

However, the format is really only the start. Sequencing does not stop there. The parts of your report where you are in full control also need a logical sequence. These include your sections, subsections, paragraphs and even the sentences within the paragraphs. We will look at this in Chapter 3.

The third principle is to write well, or at least well enough not to trouble your readers. The quality of the writing must be good enough to keep them reading and good enough not to distract them from the message. They understand all the words – and the paragraphs and sentences do not meander on and on. Your readers are busy people and will resent poor writing.

Chapter 4 and the Style Guide in Chapter 8 will help you to think about your writing and make good choices where there seems to be more than one way of doing things. As already mentioned in the Preface, many people have said that good writing is hard work, and it is.

1.2 – Three Stages: Plan, Write, Edit

Good reports do not just happen, they are planned or designed. An effective approach is to keep the planning separate from the writing and keep the writing separate from the editing: plan the report, write the draft, and then edit the draft into the final report – all as separate activities. Separating them makes the tasks easier and, usually, quicker. With long reports you may decide to do this section by section, planning a single section then writing its draft and editing it. With short reports you may instead choose to plan the entire report first and then write it all before editing it all. It is your choice.

Plan, write, edit is our version of that universal principle – design, make and test each part of something before bringing it all together. Good planning, or good designing, reduces the amount of time you are likely to spend correcting and rewriting, but there will always be some rewriting and sometimes quite a lot. This is not a factory production line so you may never get it 'right first time' as the quality gurus put it, but this book will help you to get it better first time – and that will save you time overall. Chapter 6 shows how a sample fictional report was planned, written and edited.

Consistency

Your organisation's template will dictate consistency for major design issues, such as the page layout, fonts and heading styles. But what about the relatively minor things like how to punctuate bullet points, when to put a comma before *and*, and when to hyphenate words and when not to? For such things you need a style guide not just a dictionary. Many organisations provide dictionaries, but not many provide a style guide. There is an extensive style guide with well over 200 entries in Chapter 8.

Ideally, all your organisation's reports should have a consistent layout and style – just as they all use the same logo and organisation name. It is part of your organisation's brand or image. Without a guide, different authors do things differently and there is no consistency. This is particularly important for consultancies that produce hundreds of reports a year from dozens of specialists for dozens of clients.

Sometimes the rules of grammar and punctuation can be problematic and even grammarians can argue about them. However, consistency of grammar, punctuation and style is an important principle to follow. Where there are legitimate variations, chose one and stick to it as best you can. As a trivial example: how many spaces should there be between two sentences? One or two? One thing is sure, do not cover both possibilities by alternating between one and two as I have seen people do. Decide and then apply your decision consistently. (Nowadays the preference is for one space.)

Do readers notice inconsistencies? Many notice big inconsistencies and some notice small ones. The danger, albeit slight, is that noticing becomes a slippery slope down which a few slide into asking, 'If you didn't take the trouble to get this right, how much trouble did you take to get the facts right?' At that point, those readers may start to lose trust in you and, while their views may be irritatingly pedantic, they can influence others. Even though it is a small risk try to avoid it, especially with external clients.

British v American English

We all know that there are some differences between British and American English. Thankfully, the rigours (or rigors?) of business writing impose restrictions, especially on business terminology, that make it unlikely that readers from one tradition will struggle to understand a report from the other tradition. It is things like a poor structure, lack of clarity, muddled thinking, failing to recognise what matters to readers and so on that are far more likely to hinder understanding than the small differences between British and American English. Nevertheless, some of those differences may be important at times, so they are mentioned in the text where appropriate, especially in Chapter 8, the Style Guide.

1.3 – Three Rhetorical Appeals

At its simplest, a report is a message from an author to one or more readers. Put like that it is obvious, but there are three parts to that statement and a report is effective when the three work well together: the author, the message and the readers.

People have recognised the importance of this trio since the time of the Ancient Greeks, and probably before, and they are studied in rhetoric. The trio are known as the three rhetorical appeals – three things that need to work if a message is to be persuasive. You may not have thought about it much but reports must persuade their readers to accept their recommendations. The three rhetorical appeals are called ethos, logos and pathos – not that you need to remember their names.

Ethos. The first rhetorical appeal, *ethos*, from which we get the word *ethical*, is about the author. As a reader, why should I trust you? What is your authority for writing this? Why should I listen to you? This rhetorical appeal is usually relatively easy to achieve – provided you know you should try to achieve it.

You were probably asked to do this work and write this report, or your organisation was. Maybe it is part of a contract that your organisation has won or maybe it is an internal request. That all adds to your authority and any report written by a consultancy for a client should mention the contract in some way, but there is more to it than that. When you describe how you gathered your evidence or data you are using the ethos rhetorical appeal. 'Look!' you are saying, 'See how I did it. You can trust me, I did it right. I know what I am doing.'

The specialist accuracy of the report (or robustness as we put it earlier) is also part of the ethos. Consider the opposite, if readers question how thorough the work was, if they criticise the methods you used – then you lose credibility. Also, be honest. If you have contrary evidence – present it, describe it and explain why you have discounted it (if you have). Look after the ethos rhetorical appeal. Plan for it – do not leave it to chance.

Logos. The second of the rhetorical appeals, *logos*, from which we get the word *logical*, is an appeal to reason – to the logic of your argument. Does it make sense? Is it logical? Does it hang together? This also is about robustness but this time it is about how robust your reasoning, argument or case is. Again, there is more to it. Yes, your case must be logical, but also it must be seen to be logical. Even though you believe it is logical, if the readers cannot see the logic, then it is not logical to them and your argument fails.

Here, once again, we are focussing on the arrangement or sequence of your argument. This goes from the arrangement of the major sections to the subsections, to the paragraphs and even to the sentences. Once again, do not leave it to chance – think about it and plan it. Sadly, the logical arrangement of the details in many reports is one of the most heavily criticised aspects.

Pathos. The third appeal is *pathos*, from which we get the word *empathy*, and it is an appeal to the readers and especially to their emotions. Why should they be interested in your report? Do they care? Does it matter to them? You start to answer that when you state the aims of the report, which perhaps they gave you anyway. They are interested because they asked you to do this; they have a problem and they asked you to solve it for them. Do not be reticent about gently reminding of that through how you express each aim: the aim is to solve this problem so that they get this benefit. You are reminding them of what is in it for them – the benefits. Of course, they are looking for solutions to their problems – but what they really want are the benefits they will get from those solutions. Once again, do not leave that to chance, think about and plan the pathos.

If that was helpful, then why not buy the book from your local Amazon website?

Printed in Great Britain
by Amazon